The 6 Readiness Factors
for Planning, Changing, or Advancing Your Career

Donald Whiteside

Copyright © 2021 Donald Whiteside

All rights reserved. This book or portion thereof may not be copied, reproduced, distributed, stored in a retrieval system, posted, or transmitted by any means (including, but not limited to, electronic, mechanical, photocopy, recording, or other) without prior written permission of the author. Exceptions made for brief quotations in printed reviews.

The publisher and the author are providing this book and its contents on an "as is" basis and make no representations or warranties of any kind with respect to this book or its contents. Your reliance on or use of any information contained herein is completely at your own risk and constitutes your understanding and express agreement that to the maximum extent permitted by law, the publisher, author, and/or any referenced sources shall not be liable under any circumstances for any loss or damages whatsoever, actual or perceived, regardless if due to errors, inaccuracies, omissions, or negligence. The author is not an attorney or licensed career counselor and the content contained herein is not intended to and does not constitute legal advice or professional career counseling; always consult a licensed professional when legal or other guidance is appropriate or needed. Websites, products, or services mentioned herein have not been vetted for suitability, accuracy, or correctness and are provided only as examples or references; inclusion does not imply endorsement and omission is not to be interpreted negatively. Any content, URLs, or websites cited are subject to change.

ISBN: 978-1-7372672-0-1

DEDICATION

To my wife, Sherry, for her support over the years
and extreme patience during this book project,

To my adult children, Kim, DJ, and Lisa, of whom I am so proud,
and whose own writing talents and achievements have provided inspiration,

To my sister, Janet, who first encouraged me to write a book,

And most of all, to God, for the many blessings He has provided and for always having my back.

ACKNOWLEDGEMENTS

A special thanks to my editor, Anna A., for her assistance in this project. Her editing expertise, sharp eye, and excellent suggestions resulted in a better book than would have otherwise been possible.

CONTENTS

Your New Career Path Begins Today 1
    The Career Development Process 4

Overview of the Six Readiness Factors 6
    Education (and Training) 7
    Experience 7
    Skills (and Abilities) 7
    Credentials 8
    Differentiation 8
    Interviewing 8
    Mixes and Variations of the Readiness Factors 9
    What About Self-Employment? 10

Education and Training 11
    Do I Actually Need a College Degree? 11
    What If a Degree is Required? 13
    Accreditation 14
    Education Sounds Really Hard 15
    Education is Expensive 15
    Special State Programs 17
    Is Everyone in Agreement? 17

Experience 20
    I Have the Right Experience 20
    I Have Work Experience, But Not the Amount or Specific Type Sought 21
    I Have Little or No Work Experience 23
    Your Personal Readiness: Experience 24

Skills (and Abilities) 25
    Job-Specific Skills 26
    Communication and Interpersonal Skills 26
    Physical Abilities 28
    Leadership Skills 29
    Your Personal Readiness: Skills and Abilities 30

Credentials 31
    Licensing 31

    Do I Need a License? 33

    Certification 33

    You Might Need Both 35

    Obtaining a Credential as a Condition of Employment 36

    Your Personal Readiness: Credentials 36

Differentiation 38

    Pass a Tissue, Please 38

    How Can I Differentiate Myself? 39

    Volunteer at Work 39

    Additional Credentials 40

    Speak a Second Language 40

    Read and Stay Up-to-Date 41

    Organizational Membership 41

    Attend Conferences and Seminars 42

    Become Known in Your Field 42

    Earn a Higher-Level Degree 43

    The Final Differentiation 43

    Your Personal Readiness: Differentiation 44

Interviewing (Part 1): Pre-Interview Considerations 45

    First You Have to Get an Interview 46

    What Constitutes a Good Fit? 46

    Cover Your Bases 48

    Resume or CV? 49

    Professional References 50

    If They Can't See It, They Can't Read It 53

    Transcripts Can Be Tricky 53

    Online Applications 53

    Will Your Social Media Help or Hurt? 59

    Your Personal Readiness: Interviewing 60

Interviewing (Part 2): The Interview Itself 61

    Physical Interview Logistics 61

    Go Prepared 62

    Show and Tell 63

    Interview Classification 64

    Interview Formats 64

        Face-to-Face Interview 65

- Single Interviewer 65
- Panel Interview 65
- Sequential Interview 66
- Telephone Interview 66
- Online Video Interview 66
- Text Interview 67
- Job Fair Interview 67
- Meal/Social Interview 68
- Overlap? 69
- Interview Types 69
  - Question and Answer (Q&A) 69
  - Behavioral (STAR) 70
  - Task/Problem Solving 72
  - Skills Tests 72
  - Stress Interview 74
  - Group 74
- Answering Questions 74
- It's Your Turn to Ask Questions 75
- Eye Contact Mistakes 76
- Should I Negotiate Salary During the Interview? 77
- Ageism and the Older Applicant 77
- Your Personal Readiness: Interviewing 79

Interviewing (Part 3): After the Interview 80
- Debrief 80
- Thank the Interviewers 80
- What If You Didn't Get the Job? 81

Self-Assessment of the Readiness Factors 83
- Education Self-Assessment 83
- Experience Self-Assessment 86
- Skills Self-Assessment 87
- Credentials Self-Assessment 88
- Differentiation Self-Assessment 89
- Interviewing Self-Assessment 91

Creating Your Individual Development Plan (IDP) 93
- Developing "Smart" Goals for Your IDP 93
- Military Resources 94

    Individual Development Plan for Education/Training 94

    Individual Development Plan for Experience 97

    Individual Development Plan for Skills 99

    Individual Development Plan for Credentials 101

    Individual Development Plan for Differentiation 104

    Individual Development Plan for Interviewing 105

Go for It! 106

Appendix A: Telephone and Online Video Interviews 107

    Telephone Interviews 107

    Online Video Interviews 108

        Location 108

        Technology 109

        Photographic Considerations 110

        Background 110

        Lighting 110

        Camera Angle 112

        Camera-to-Subject Distance 112

        Glare 112

        Clothing 113

        On-Camera Conduct 113

    Practice 113

Appendix B: Sample Behavioral Questions 114

    Teamwork 114

    Customer Service 114

    Honesty/Integrity 115

    Conflict 115

    Cultural Diversity 115

    Judgement/Resourcefulness/Problem Solving 115

    Multitasking/Stress 115

    Leadership/Management 116

    Attitudes About Work and Self 116

Appendix C: Negotiating a Starting Salary 118

References 122

About the Author 123

Your New Career Path Begins Today

Ask yourself, "Am I happy with my career?"

Everyone will, at some point, ask themselves this question. Students in high school or college who are still planning their careers or about to enter the workforce may wonder whether they are adequately prepared. Some individuals may toil at jobs needed for income but don't find the work itself particularly interesting or satisfying. Perhaps the pay is also less than satisfactory, and they feel the time has come to completely change careers. Others may be working in their chosen field but feel their careers have stagnated. The excitement which initially drew them to this field in the first place has diminished somewhat, and now they want to advance their careers through new challenges and responsibilities.

Where do you stand? Consider the following statements:

- I am a student still planning my career.
- I am a recent graduate looking to secure a job in my chosen field.
- I already have a job, but I want a *career*.
- I am already working in my chosen field, but feel somewhat trapped in my current position and would like to advance my career.

Do any of these statements describe your current situation? If so, then be prepared to start on a new and life-changing path, one designed to plan, change, or advance your career. How will this happen?

- First, this book will introduce you to the six readiness factors critical to successfully achieving your career goals.
- Next, we will assess your personal readiness regarding each factor.
- Finally, you will develop an Individual Development Plan (IDP), your blueprint for success in improving your readiness.

About this book:

- It is not just another motivational book on pursuing careers. Think of it as a *tactical planning guide for your career*.
- It is not intended to help you decide *which* career field is right for you. It assumes you already know what you want in a career and offers a realistic, logical approach to reaching that goal.
- Additionally, it provides detailed and practical guidance designed to improve your success at job interviews, whether in-person or online. These suggestions are not based on my personal preferences but on insight I have gained through decades of observing and participating in actual job interviews, noticing the incredible number and types of avoidable mistakes made all too frequently by candidates. My intent is to provide you with the benefit of that insight and enable you to avoid those same disastrous mistakes.

An executive I know prominently displays a sign in her office which reads:

Dreams + Inaction = Squat

Yes, it is important to have dreams regarding your career. Dreams provide hope and help you envision an end goal. However, failing to take the actions necessary to make a dream become a reality guarantees it will never be anything more than a wishful fantasy. As the sign states, without action, you end up with "squat."

The need to take action sounds obvious and simple enough, but following through and actually taking the necessary action always requires commitment, hard work, and usually some amount of sacrifice.

Consider the career pursuits of my friend—let's call him Tyler—who worked for a large corporation. For years, Tyler's career goal was to secure a well-paying position in management. As is often the case, a bachelor's degree was the minimum level of education required by his employer to apply for any management position. Although he had previously attended college full-time and accumulated about two years' worth of credit hours, Tyler never finished or earned a degree. With a career goal now in mind, he decided to resume his education and start taking courses on a part-time basis. Tyler figured that within just a few years, the required degree would be in hand and he would then qualify for any promotional opportunities which may arise. He had a dream and formulated a plan to take action. So far, so good.

Unfortunately, after just a few semesters, Tyler quickly grew tired of the difficult and seemingly endless routine of taking classes and doing homework while working full-time. He also became increasingly sidetracked with various after-work recreational team sports activities. Whatever the season, there was a sport Tyler enjoyed playing. Eventually, he dropped his continuing education efforts altogether in favor of participating in sports.

Yet, just as before, whenever promotional or management opportunities were posted by his employer, Tyler continued to grumble about the bachelor's degree requirement. This all seemed very unfair to him as he possessed the experience and other qualifications needed for these positions but simply lacked the degree. Year after year, he complained, all while continuing to spend his evenings playing sports. In the end, Tyler never did complete the bachelor's degree. He also never received the promotion he sought and was relegated to watching from the sidelines as opportunities regularly passed him by.

After observing his situation for a few years, something occurred to me. If Tyler had simply put the recreational sports on hold—just for a while—and worked aggressively towards completing the degree, by now, he could have had both the higher-paying management position he dreamed of and still been able to play sports. He literally could have had it all!

This is a classic example of an individual having a career dream
but not taking the action necessary to make it a reality.

Consider your own situation. Does achieving your career goal require obtaining something you are currently missing? Perhaps meeting a specific educational requirement, acquiring a particular license or certification, learning a specialized skill, or gaining certain work experience? If so, are you prepared to leave your comfort zone and overcome the obstacles preventing you from achieving your career dream?

The decision to take action—I mean *really* take action—can be very intimidating. The challenge of making your dreams become a reality is never an easy, passive undertaking. Depending on your particular goals and situation, the time frame required could be relatively short or may even take several years. However, if you want to achieve your dreams badly enough, you have to decide to take that first step!

It is easy to feel overwhelmed because the task ahead simply looks too hard. But you can do this! How? You may have heard the phrase:

How do you eat an elephant? One bite at a time.

The next time you see a skyscraper, stop and think about the incredible amount of work and diversity of tasks involved in constructing that building. To the average person, such an undertaking might seem almost inconceivable, yet skyscrapers are regularly built all over the world. How are such ventures accomplished?

The project manager takes the exceedingly complex process of constructing a huge building and breaks it down into smaller, more manageable pieces. Each smaller piece of the overall project is carefully and logically planned and then carried out, step by step. The bottom line and key to success is that the project manager has a detailed plan.

With a clear plan to guide your career, you will find that each challenge and necessary action can also be broken down into smaller, more manageable pieces. Sure, each task will require hard work, but never lose sight of the fact that your effort will pay off tremendously in the end by providing lifelong benefits. In addition to being financial in nature, these benefits will result in personal satisfaction. Just think—you will be where you want to be, doing what you want to do, all while being appropriately compensated.

Watch out! Some people fall into the self-defeating trap of blaming someone or something else for their lack of career success. Before moving ahead, allow me to share a fact that may be difficult for some to hear.

YOU and ONLY YOU are responsible for your career.
Nobody except YOU really cares about your career advancement.

Yes, this sounds rather cold. However, years of observation and experience have repeatedly proven it to be true. Regardless of how you think the world ought to be, the reality is that you are the only one who really cares about your career and can change or advance it. Sure, supervisors, coworkers, teachers, friends, and others may help, mentor, offer development or training programs, provide opportunities for advancement, or assist in some other way—as they should! However, in the end, it is all up to you.

But wait! What if others are, in fact, at least in some way responsible for adversely affecting your career? Maybe your current boss is, in fact, a real jerk. Perhaps you attended a lousy high school where quality learning was next to impossible. You may have had issues with your parents, spouse, or ex-spouse. Life may have really handed you some bad breaks.

Some or even all of these factors might have contributed to your current situation. However, while you can't change the past, you can control what you do moving forward, thereby changing the future. Don't let yesterday's setbacks become excuses for inaction today, causing you to remain stuck. Even if someone or something else did help derail your career progress, you're the one who now has to find a way to get back on track.

How does one plan a career? Think about what happens when traveling on an airplane. While you are boarding and getting situated, the pilot and co-pilot are busy in the cockpit preparing the plane for takeoff. They do this by using a preflight checklist, a set of specific steps to be followed to ensure the craft is airworthy. The list involves checking numerous equipment settings such as flap and rudder positions, fuel level, hydraulic pressures, etc. Each item is individually and deliberately checked before the plane ever attempts to head down the runway.

Although the pilots may be experienced professionals who have logged thousands of flight hours and operated this aircraft model for years, they still go through the preflight checklist, line-by-line, before each and every flight. Why? Aside from government regulations requiring them to do so, using a checklist ensures nothing will be missed, forgotten, overlooked, or left to chance. By completing the preflight checklist, the pilots know every critical aspect of the aircraft has been double-checked and the flight will be able to proceed safely.

Similarly, career preparation requires specific parameters to be double-checked if a job search or career change is to "take off" successfully. I refer to these as the ***Six Readiness Factors***. The six readiness factors are:

- Education
- Experience
- Skills
- Credentials
- Differentiation
- Interviewing

This book will examine each readiness factor and assist you in thinking through them as you prepare. Of course, not every readiness factor will apply to every job, career situation, or individual in the same way or to the same extent. Recent college graduates and those changing careers may require significant preparation for every factor. On the other hand, working individuals looking to advance their existing careers may be surprised to find themselves already well prepared, with only a few factors requiring attention. However, like the preflight checklist, examining each factor will help ensure that nothing regarding the pursuit of your career goal will be missed, forgotten, overlooked, or left to chance.

THE CAREER DEVELOPMENT PROCESS

As you will see, the readiness factors are essential components in the overall career development process. The process itself (shown below) is logical, straightforward, and easy to understand. How does it work, and where do you begin?

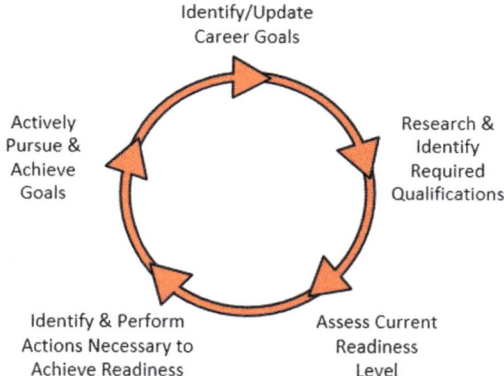

You already completed the first step of the process when you identified your career goals. This may have been as basic as selecting the field in which you wish to work. Perhaps you decided to move into an entirely new career field altogether. Or, your goal may be to advance your current career by pursuing a higher-level position or moving into management.

Next, it will be necessary to research the qualifications for the chosen career. The six factors provide a framework for examining readiness relative to both the requirements themselves and interview preparedness. After all, merely meeting the minimum job qualifications will not be enough. Excellent interviewing skills are necessary to successfully secure the desired position.

You will then perform a self-assessment to determine your current readiness level regarding each of the six factors. Most individuals typically find they need to further develop and prepare themselves for at least some of the factors, and the self-assessment tool will help identify what needs to be done. Finally, you will develop an action plan that serves as a "to-do" list for improving your readiness.

"By failing to prepare, you are preparing to fail."

- Benjamin Franklin

After you have reached an improved state of readiness, it is finally time to make your goal a reality. At this point in the process, you should be going on job interviews, or better yet, actually landing that job or promotion you were seeking. Once your immediate career goal has been reached, the entire process is repeated. Career development is not merely a one-shot effort, but a continual process designed to keep your career advancing.

The upcoming chapters will discuss each individual readiness factor in detail. Are you ready to make a significant change and take that first step toward a new or improved career and life? Great! Move on to the next chapter!

Overview of the Six Readiness Factors

Just as pilots need to prepare their aircraft for takeoff, you also will have to plan and prepare to successfully attain your dream job or new career. This preparation process will require an honest self-evaluation regarding the six different but related and essential readiness factors. Of course, the mix and depth of the readiness factors will differ for every person, situation, and career field. Some individuals will need to fully address every factor; others, perhaps fewer or to a lesser degree.

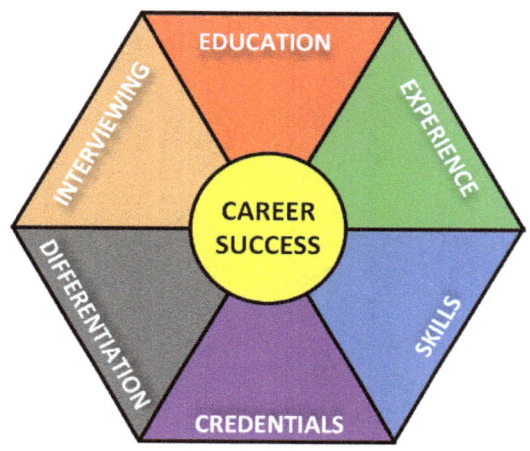

The first four factors (**E**ducation, **E**xperience, **S**kills, and **C**redentials) relate primarily to the prerequisites for working in a particular career field. The last two factors (**D**ifferentiation and **I**nterviewing) focus on enhancing success in the application and interviewing process. To help remember the six factors, think of the first letter of each word in the following simple phrase:

Every Employer Seeks Competent and Dependable Individuals

This chapter will briefly examine each readiness factor. The following chapters follow will explore each in considerably more depth and detail.

I should point out that some professionals, most notably those in the human resources and recruitment fields, may make a technical distinction between the terms "applicant" and "candidate." An applicant is an individual who has formally applied for employment but who has not yet been selected for further consideration. On the other hand, a candidate is an applicant whom the employer has decided to interview and actively consider. Despite this difference, in many companies, other professionals and managers frequently use the terms interchangeably. Rather than continually distinguishing between them, this book will simply use the two terms interchangeably.

EDUCATION (AND TRAINING)

Most, but not all, fields of employment usually require a certain amount of formal education or training up front. In some fields, a specific amount or type of education may even be necessary before one can legally work or be considered for employment. Typical educational or training requirements might include a high school diploma or equivalent (at a minimum), a two or four-year college degree, or completion of an apprenticeship or non-degree certificate program.

If a college degree is a prerequisite, it may need to be in a specific major, such as engineering, accounting, education, nursing, or physics. Sometimes, it is not enough to merely have the required degree; the college program awarding the degree may also need to have a particular "accreditation", such as ABET (for engineering) or AACSB (for business). Accreditation will be discussed in detail in a later chapter.

Training might include completing a certificate or non-degree program, such as that for a medical assistant or beautician. It may also involve obtaining in-depth, specialized training on specific software, instrumentation, machinery, or equipment. Some fields are highly regulated and may require individuals to have a working knowledge of current and relevant federal, state, or local laws, as well as applicable standards and codes.

No doubt, education requires perhaps more resources than any other factor. Not only can it be financially burdensome, but it consumes limited time resources and may also impact your job or people who play an important role in your life. Plus, what if you currently have no college or special training? At first, you might think satisfying any educational requirement is simply out of reach, but don't give up. The Education and Training chapter offers some suggestions for possible resources and ways to approach this.

EXPERIENCE

Except for some entry-level or training positions, employers almost always expect applicants to have prior work experience. This is understandable as experience serves as evidence of your skills and ability to perform the work. It also usually enables a new employee to become productive more quickly and minimizes training costs. If you have the needed experience, you should be prepared to speak knowledgeably about it, providing sufficient details if needed.

But what if you have little or no work experience, or what you do have is not relevant to the position sought? The Experience chapter suggests some approaches for this situation.

SKILLS (AND ABILITIES)

Perhaps you know people who made it through their college education or training program, but did not really get very much out of it. Remember that student in your class who slept most of the time but still was able to barely pass with a D-grade? If so, you would probably agree that education and training alone do not necessarily translate into functional skill sets.

This gap between the completion of education and the resulting actual skill level is why "skills" are identified as a factor distinctly separate from education. Just because someone takes an art class does not guarantee they can immediately function as a landscape oil painter or technical illustrator. One year of piano lessons does not result in the skill necessary to perform as a concert pianist. No, such skills usually take years to develop and master long after the foundational education or training itself has been completed.

For example, in the field of electronics, a technician must have the skill and ability to read schematic diagrams, solder wires and components, and proficiently operate digital multimeters, oscilloscopes, and other specialized devices. Machinists and die makers must know how to use and accurately read micrometers and dial indicators. These are instruments that most people have never used, or perhaps even knew existed. A nursing assistant needs the skill to use medical terminology correctly and take blood pressure, pulse, and pulse oximeter readings accurately. In every field, truly skilled individuals can perform their tasks properly and safely, every time, without making mistakes, causing waste, or requiring rework. Just because a person knows how such a task should be done does not mean the individual possesses the actual skill to do it properly on a consistent basis.

Additionally, some career fields, such as law enforcement or firefighting, require specific physical skills and abilities. Applicants may need to demonstrate a baseline level of physical fitness and agility by performing a certain number of exercises or completing a series of timed tasks.

Finally, this readiness factor also includes so-called "soft" skills, such as communication and interpersonal skills. While most would agree these skills are especially critical in career areas such as sales, they are, in fact, necessary for success in any field. A later chapter will explore how soft skills enter into the mix for career success.

CREDENTIALS

Some career fields may prefer or even require possession of a specific license, certification, trade level (e.g., journeyperson, formerly known as "journeyman"), or other such designation. If legally permitted, some employers may be willing to hire an individual who does not have the credential at the time of hire, but will require it be obtained within a specified time frame as a condition for keeping the job. The process of earning credentials may involve completing multiple steps or phases while acquiring the work experience necessary for the final license or certification. The Credentials chapter will discuss this topic in detail, explaining their purpose and who issues them.

DIFFERENTIATION

The Differentiation readiness factor is one you may not have previously thought about or even knew existed. Suppose you have worked really hard to ensure you have the right education, work experience, skills, and credentials for the job you seek. Excellent!

However, stop for a moment and put yourself in the shoes of the people conducting the interview. When interviewers look into a waiting room of job candidates, what do they see? More often than not, they see a group of unknown individuals, clone-like applicants who all essentially have the same degree and work experience. All their resumes and cover letters are nicely prepared. If a license or certification is required, they have it. Finally, they all are dressed well and appropriately. How can an interviewer choose?

At the most basic level, interviewing is a situation where you are selling or marketing yourself. The goal is to convince the interviewer that, compared to all the other available candidates, you are the best choice. But how can this be accomplished when all the choices available to the interviewer seem to be similar if not almost identical?

In the marketing field, making one's product or service stand out as the best choice from among other comparable options is known as *differentiation*. The goal of differentiation is to convince a buyer that a specific product or service is different enough from the offerings of all other competitors that it is clearly the best and only logical choice. In a job interview scenario, the "buyer" is the interviewer and you are the "product" being offered. The critical question to answer is:

What do you offer that the other candidates do not,
thereby clearly making you the best choice?

Fortunately, there are ways to differentiate yourself from the other applicants, and these will be discussed in a later chapter.

INTERVIEWING

All career preparation efforts will have been wasted if your job interview does not go well. Occasionally, an interview may be unsuccessful due to unrealistic expectations on the part of the individual interviewer. Other times, there may have simply been a very large pool of exceptionally well-qualified applicants. That may be good news for the employer, who has plenty of choices in this situation, but not for all the interviewees who were passed by without a job offer. More often than not, however, failure to receive a job offer is likely the result of how the candidate handled the interview.

Candidates are often surprised when they discover employers sometimes include a written test or other demonstration of proficiency as part of the interview process. This aspect of the interview helps weed out the golden-tongued candidates who may talk a good line, but in reality cannot do the job because they are deficient in the necessary skills. An employer who has been fooled once by such a candidate will typically learn from that experience and thereafter implement a more reliable method of assessing the real abilities of those being interviewed. Do not assume this approach to evaluating candidates applies only to lower or entry-level positions; it does not. Do you have a job interview coming up? Do you know if the interview will involve a demonstration of proficiency?

The number of formats and types of job interviews one may face is extensive and may appear in various combinations. To prepare you for whatever comes your way, we will discuss each of these in detail. Having performed hundreds of job interviews and myself interviewed for numerous positions, I know what it is like to sit on either side of the interview table. My goal is to help you go into that interview prepared and ready to perform in such a way that a job offer will be yours.

This factor involves many aspects relating to before, during, and after the interview. There are so many, in fact, that three separate chapters are dedicated to discussing interviewing in detail.

MIXES AND VARIATIONS OF THE READINESS FACTORS

As you would expect, every individual's career path is unique. Therefore, for each person, the individual factors will be emphasized to varying degrees. The readiness factors still apply, but sometimes just in different ways.

The distinction between readiness factors may also start to blur at times. For example, students in nursing, laboratory technology, radiologic (X-ray) technology, physical therapy, nutrition, and various other medical fields are typically required to gain hands-on experience through internships or clinical rotations. While participating in these activities, the students may be paid or unpaid and usually receive formal college credit for working the prescribed number of hours and successfully completing the program. Therefore, should this be classified as education, skill development, or both? It likely will not count as "work experience", per se, as most employers typically do not consider clinical training or internships as such. These individuals were not hired as a regular employees but are present in a learning capacity. Although these students may perform some of the duties of an employee, they must work under the oversight of an experienced and credentialed professional.

Thus, although the distinction between readiness factors may occasionally become fuzzy, this is not an issue and does not in any way diminish the importance of the factors. As you can see, each factor may be viewed differently or in combinations, but nonetheless, they are all somehow addressed.

An interesting career path that may, at least at first, appear to somewhat mix up the readiness factors is one involving a skilled trade apprenticeship. Apprenticeship programs are the norm when seeking to enter careers such as those for electricians, plumbers, tool and die makers, HVAC, carpenters, and many others. These programs differ in that they initially address the readiness factors in reverse order! Unlike typical careers, where one must already have all the prerequisite education, experience, skills, and credentials before even being considered for employment, an apprenticeship places the application and interview process up front. Once accepted into a multi-year apprenticeship program, the individual then typically receives:

- Some amount of formal education by taking prescribed college or other courses (although the courses may or may not be applicable toward a degree)
- Hands-on work experience under the oversight of an experienced tradesperson
- On-the-job training to develop the specific skills needed
- A credential for the field of work, such as a journeyperson card, upon successful completion of all program requirements
- The experience plus the credential may, in some fields, then lead to a license (another credential)

Apprenticeships are an exceptional opportunity, especially when one considers the formal education component is usually provided without cost to the student. Additionally, apprentices gain experience and learn the required skills all while being paid a reasonable wage, and in the end, are frequently assured employment in a well-paying job.

Note, however, that although the readiness factors may have initially been in reverse order when entering the field, once the apprenticeship is complete and the journey-level tradesperson is in the workforce, the situation typically changes back to normal. Suppose the tradesperson decides a few years later to seek employment elsewhere with a different company or specialize in a specific area of the field. In this case, most of the readiness factors would apply just as they would for any other jobseeker. The exception might be a situation where, for example, construction tradespeople work out of a union hall and are assigned to various contractors on a rotational basis. Otherwise, someone working in the trades will need to compete with other candidates for an open position. When that occurs, the readiness factors come into play once again and can assist the candidate in getting the job.

WHAT ABOUT SELF-EMPLOYMENT?

Not all career paths necessarily involve working as an employee for a company or other organization. According to the U.S. Bureau of Labor Statistics (BLS), the percentage of self-employed American workers was about 10% in 2015[1]. This percentage has declined slightly over the past two decades, down from about 12% in 1994.

A person considering self-employment may wonder whether the readiness factors play any role in their career plans. The answer is a resounding "Yes." While this book may be primarily directed to those seeking a position as an employee, knowledge of the readiness factors is also very applicable and useful to individuals pursuing self-employment.

Consider the following:

- Many self-employed professions (e.g., physician, lawyer, dentist, accountant, etc.) require education consisting of a college degree.
- Working in the trades (electrician, plumber, carpenter, etc.) usually requires specialized training, such as that acquired through an apprenticeship.
- While some self-employed careers (e.g., artist, photographer, writer, etc.) may not have specific educational or degree requirements, most individuals in those fields utilize some type of additional training to enhance their knowledge and abilities.
- Experience may be even more critical when self-employed. What client wants to hire an inexperienced carpenter, wedding photographer, tax preparer, etc.?
- Skill is often what the self-employed are actually selling.
- Credentials such as licenses (especially for professions and trades) may be prerequisites to working in particular fields. Certifications (e.g., designation as a Master of Photography) may be a differentiating factor in attracting clients.
- How does the self-employed individual differentiate themselves? Why should a client choose you over other service or product providers?
- In the realm of self-employment, "interviewing" translates to "selling."

As you can see, the readiness factors are definitely applicable, although in a slightly different way. The self-employed individual utilizes the factors not to land a job with an employer but to enter a particular field and successfully attract clients.

Education and Training

Every position in every organization either has or should have a corresponding formal, written job description. Although the format of job descriptions may vary significantly from organization to organization, these documents, at a minimum, describe and detail the:

- Various responsibilities and duties of the position
- Knowledge, skills, and abilities (often referred to as KSAs) necessary to perform the job
- Minimum education, training, and work experience an applicant must possess

When an employment opportunity is posted, the posting may include the job description, either in part or in whole, or often provide it through an online link. The latter approach allows the posting to be brief but still enables a potential applicant to review the complete (and perhaps lengthy) official job description.

In order to be considered for the open position, an applicant must meet the minimum level of education and training required as stated in the job description. In most cases, if the minimum requirements are not met, the application is immediately rejected and receives no further consideration. Education and training requirements vary considerably from position to position and field to field, but almost always include one or more of the following:

- A high school diploma or equivalent (e.g., GED)
- Completion of a non-degree education or training program (e.g., certificate)
- Completion of a formal apprenticeship
- Associate degree (e.g., AA., AS.)
- Bachelor's (or Baccalaureate) degree (e.g., BA, BS)
- Master's degree (e.g., MA, MS, MBA)
- Doctoral degree (e.g., PhD, ScD, DBA)
- Professional degree (e.g., JD, MD, DDS, DVM)

When considering a new career field or trying to advance within your current one, the minimum educational and training requirements can leave you feeling as if you have just run into a brick wall. This is especially true when a college degree is required. Often, the stated educational requirement is the first thing individuals look at when considering a new position. They almost view it as a red light/green light, signaling whether a career in that field is even possible for them. For many, that is the end of it. Discouraged, their pursuit of a career change or advancement goes no further. However, like going to the gym, little effort yields little reward.

DO I ACTUALLY NEED A COLLEGE DEGREE?

First, determine whether a college degree is actually an absolute requirement for achieving your particular career goal. True, having a degree will usually enable you to pursue more opportunities than not having one. Plus, college graduates typically earn more money over their lifetime than those with only a high school diploma. However, pursuing a traditional college education isn't necessarily for everyone, and in some cases, may not even be required. Consider the following:

- Some employers may accept work experience as a substitute for formal education.
- Programs such as apprenticeships typically incorporate any required formal education into the program itself.
- Certain fields or positions may require completion of a non-degree training program or possession of a specific credential (license, certification, etc.) rather than a degree.

As indicated above, it is not uncommon for employers to sometimes accept relevant work experience as a substitute for part or all of the stated educational requirements. How do you find out? Read the job posting or description. The requirements may permit various options, as shown in the excerpts from real job postings below:

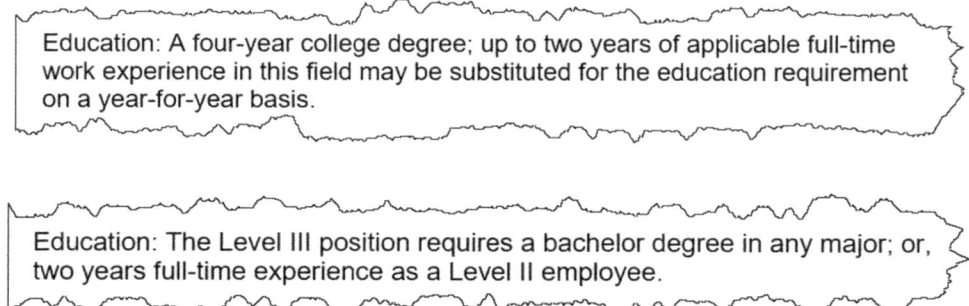

In the first example, the employer is willing to consider a candidate who does not possess a degree but has a mix of college and work experience. This particular employer will substitute work experience for up to two years of college on a year-for-year basis. In this case, a candidate without a degree but who has two years of college and two years of work experience is eligible to apply for the position.

The second example is common in positions that are part of a "job series" or progression. Such a structure usually involves a hierarchy consisting of multiple levels or tiers for related positions, such as Analyst I, II, and III. Employers often use this approach to ensure a promotional career path is available to current employees who are excellent workers but simply lack a degree. It also enables managers to attract and offer a competitive wage to highly desirable but non-degreed external candidates.

What if you currently have no college or only a few credits? A strategy in this situation might be to apply for an entry-level position (such as a Level I) that may not require a degree. Once hired, you could then work for the length of time necessary to become eligible for advancement to the next higher level. It is important to note, however, that this approach has some limitations. For example, should you later wish to pursue a higher-level position or management, such promotions will usually require a degree at some point, and the employer may not be willing to allow exceptions. A smart move might be to pursue any required degree while working and moving up through the ranks. That way, when the need arises, you will be ready.

Some training programs (e.g., apprenticeships) may not have any educational prerequisites other than a high school diploma or equivalent. Check the website or application materials for the desired apprenticeship program to find out the specific educational requirements. Also, determine whether applying to the program requires a written test, as many do. If you know your skills in a tested subject area (such as math) are not what they should be, you may wish to take a refresher or test preparation class. If these are not available, at least study on your own. Self-study books are available on various topics, and for some trades, pre-apprentice test study guides are available to help you prepare. Apprenticeship programs are very competitive, and acceptance is often based heavily on application test scores. Solid preparation for these tests is critical to help maximize your chances of gaining entry to a program.

Finally, some career fields may place more emphasis on completion of a training program or possession of a specific license or other credential than on a college degree. For example, a medical clinic looking to hire an X-ray technician might be looking for an individual who has completed a training program and is a registered radiologic technologist (registration is a credential; these will be discussed in a later chapter). In this case, having a bachelor's degree would not be of any help if the candidate lacks the specific training and registry credential. Similarly, in order to service or maintain certain radio equipment (such as in the aviation and maritime radio services), possession of a commercial General Radiotelephone Operator License issued by the United States Federal Communications Commission (FCC) is legally required. Applicants without the license would not be eligible to be employed in such a capacity regardless of how many college degrees they may have on their resumes.

WHAT IF A DEGREE IS REQUIRED?

If you find a degree is an absolute requirement to enter into a particular field or to advance within your current one, and you are committed to pursuing this career, you will obviously need to begin or complete your college education. However, before signing up for courses at a local college, extension campus, or online, you need to carefully investigate the following:

- Which degree level is needed (e.g., associate, bachelor's, etc.)?
- Is the degree required at the time of application for the job, or will currently enrolled students also be considered?
- Does the degree need to be specific (e.g., accounting, mechanical engineering, microbiology, etc.), or can it be general in nature (e.g., liberal arts)?
- Does the college program granting the degree need to have a specific accreditation?

The number of possible degrees is almost overwhelming and their names can be very confusing. Additionally, not all degrees are created equal, and every job posting and employer might have different expectations. For example, a position requiring a "Bachelor of Science in Electrical Engineering (BSEE)" will probably not consider applicants with a "Bachelor of Applied Science (BAS) in Electrical Engineering Technology" degree. The latter is a hybrid degree, typically awarded in an "associate degree + two years" program. Such programs usually enable a graduate of a community college to apply the credits earned from the associate degree toward a general, four-year bachelor's degree from a larger university. While both are bachelor's degrees and appear to involve electrical engineering, they are not considered equal.

How specific must the degree be? Some job descriptions have educational requirements which are extremely specific while others are somewhat more flexible and will consider applicants with related degrees. Shown below is an excerpt from an actual job description for a Manufacturing Engineer posted online by an employer.

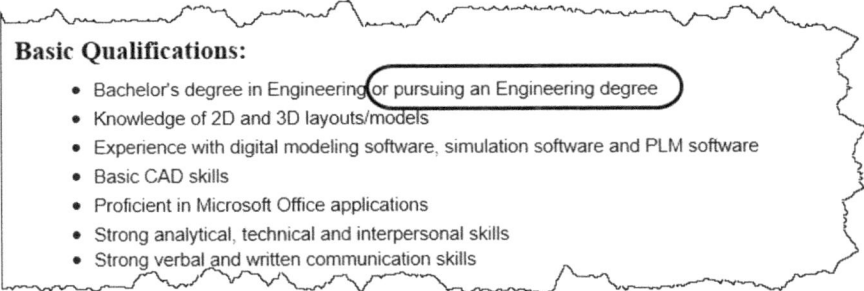

This position permits applicants to have a bachelor's degree in any type of engineering (e.g., electrical, mechanical, chemical, etc.). However, the employer will also consider a student currently enrolled in an engineering program (see the phrase I have circled for emphasis). Compare this to the educational requirement for a Mechanical Engineer position posted by a different employer (see below).

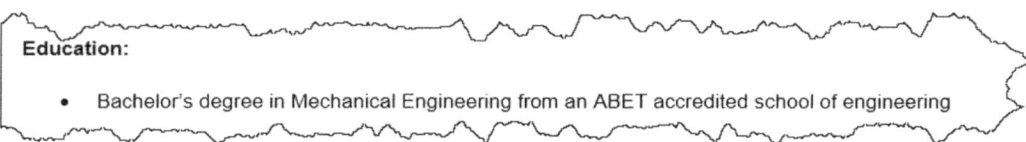

Note this particular employer not only requires the bachelor's degree to be specifically in mechanical engineering, but additionally, the degree must be issued by a college which has an ABET-accredited engineering program (ABET is an acronym for the Accreditation Board for Engineering and Technology, Inc.). What exactly is accreditation and how does a college program become accredited?

ACCREDITATION

In some fields, simply having the specified degree is not enough. The degree must also be from a college which has been accredited by a particular organization. Accreditation is a process whereby a college voluntarily goes through a rigorous review by an independent, outside party. The review is intended to verify that the college, its professors, and course curriculum meet the standards of quality set forth by the entity granting the accreditation.

If the review determines the college is in compliance with the requirements and standards, it is then recognized as being accredited. Accreditation is usually awarded for a specific period of time after which the review process must be repeated. The process of accreditation is time-consuming and expensive for colleges, usually involving an on-site inspection (which might last several days) by representatives of the accrediting body. In the end, it is not just prestigious for a college to have accredited educational programs; it also gives the school a competitive edge in attracting new students.

Who are these accrediting entities? Numerous accrediting bodies exist, and with only a few exceptions, it is important to learn whether the accrediting organization is recognized by the U.S. Department of Education (USDE) or the Council for Higher Education Accreditation (CHEA). Note that the USDE does not accredit the college or educational program itself; rather, it recognizes accrediting entities which it deems to be reliable authorities of educational quality in a specific field. If a college is accredited by an entity not recognized by the USDE, students attending that college may not be eligible for federally provided financial aid. To learn more about the role of the USDE in the accreditation process, visit their website at http://www.ed.gov/accreditation.

To further complicate matters, it may not be enough that a college is accredited. It is important to know exactly which programs at the college are covered by the accreditation and to identify the accrediting entity. Some accreditation programs apply to an institution overall and may be helpful in separating legitimate colleges from the shady "diploma mills" that issue "degrees" to anyone willing to pay. The primary goal of these so-called "colleges" is usually to take your money, and in return, provide you with an easy-to-get degree of dubious value, requiring little or no work on your part and backed by no real education. Sure, you may receive a fancy diploma, but the pretend degrees from such charlatans may not even be recognized by or acceptable to some employers.

It is not uncommon for programs or courses of study within a college to each be accredited individually. This is because accrediting entities are typically specialized organizations, each recognized within their own particular field or industry. For example, just because a college is accredited in engineering does not mean it is accredited for programs in the medical field. Similarly, just because a college is accredited in one particular medical field does not necessarily mean it is accredited in others. For example, a college nursing program may be accredited by the Commission on Collegiate Nursing Education, whereas a Physical Therapist or Physical Therapist Assistant program may be accredited by the American Physical Therapy Association Commission on Accreditation in Physical Therapy Education. These are very different accrediting bodies for very different fields of study, even though they are both medical in nature.

So, if you decide to pursue a degree, what do you need to do to ensure your time and money are well spent?

- First, as the old saying goes, if it sounds too good to be true, it is. Any offer of a college degree requiring little actual effort or time, so long as you pay, is a scam. Period.
- Second, the ultimate goal of your career plan is employment in the job or field you have chosen. Therefore, it only makes sense to determine what education the employers in this field expect applicants to possess. This may be done by reviewing job descriptions and postings for positions of interest from numerous potential employers. Knowing the minimum educational requirements stated in these documents will be essential in planning the amount and type of education you need. If a position requires college or program accreditation, the posting will usually (but not always) specify the name of the accrediting body. You may find that accreditation is required, merely desirable, or perhaps plays no role in your specific situation.
- Shop around. Colleges really do compete for your business and many have programs tailored specifically for students who work full-time. Programs may be available completely online or consist of a hybrid of both online and in-person learning. The cost of tuition and fees can also vary considerably from institution to institution, private versus public, etc.
- You may be able to complete a portion (perhaps up to two years) of the required education at a local, less expensive community college before transferring the credits to a more expensive university. The key, however, is to find out up front if, which, and how many credits will be transferable. Consult with an admissions representative at the university from which you ultimately expect to receive the final degree so there are no surprises later.
- Finally, visit the U.S. Department of Education (USDE) Database of Accredited Postsecondary Institutions and Programs (DAPIP) at http://ope.ed.gov/accreditation/Search.aspx. This is an online resource that will assist you in searching for institutions accredited in particular programs or searching for programs accredited by certain entities.

EDUCATION SOUNDS REALLY HARD

Education is perhaps the most intimidating of all the readiness factors for a number of good reasons. After all, education:

- Is expensive
- Requires time and often disrupts one's personal life
- Usually involves a multi-year commitment
- Involves hard work
- Can be humbling (can I really make it through all those challenging courses?)

It is very easy to look at the above list and quickly decide that meeting any educational requirement is just too much to handle. This might be especially tempting for individuals already working full-time or who have family responsibilities. Trust me, you are not the first person in such a situation. Many people have decided they wanted to make a major change in their lives and accepted the challenge—and went on to succeed. Don't let potential issues become excuses for inaction. Most obstacles can usually be overcome with planning and hard work. Allowing them to automatically halt the pursuit of your goals means you are willing to simply give up without a fight. Improving your career is a life-changing prospect with the potential for lifelong benefits. Isn't the reward worth the effort?

EDUCATION IS EXPENSIVE

True, education and training can be expensive. However, it is important and helpful to develop a positive mindset and think of education not as a dreaded expense, but as an investment opportunity—an investment in yourself—and one which has the potential to pay handsomely for many years to come. You probably have heard the old adage, "You have to spend money to make money," and this may well be one of those situations. But where does one get the money to make this investment? Consider the following possible resources:

- Self
- Scholarships (merit-based financial aid which does not have to be repaid)
- Grants (financial aid which does not have to be repaid)
- Employer Educational Support Programs
- Union Educational Support Programs
- Apprenticeships
- Veterans Benefits and Programs
- State/Federal Programs
- Loans (last resort)

In many cases, you may be able to utilize a mix of resources to help minimize your personal out-of-pocket expenses. You may be eligible for a grant or scholarship from a college, and perhaps your current employer or union has some type of educational support program. Leave no stone unturned when pursuing possible financial help, especially that which doesn't have to be paid back.

When looking at the availability of your own resources, consider that if changing your career path is really important to you, other nonessential things in your personal life may have to be delayed for now. Can the purchase of a newer car wait? Is purchasing a new gaming computer or larger flat-screen TV worth sacrificing attainment of your career goals?

Consult with the financial aid office at the colleges you are considering, as they will be knowledgeable about the types of scholarships, grants, and other financial aid available to their students and the requirements for each. Your local geographic area may have scholarships established by businesses or prominent philanthropic individuals. Again, the financial aid office will be able to guide you to the numerous resources available. Some types of aid may be:

- Based solely on the financial need of the student
- Based on past or current academic performance (such as outstanding high school grades) and/or other merit (such as involvement in community service)
- Limited specifically to students in a particular college major (e.g., art, biology, etc.)
- Targeted to individuals of a particular ethnicity or heritage

The typical list of available scholarships or grants is very large and you will need to carefully sift through it to see which ones may be applicable to your situation. If you are currently employed, your employer and/or labor union may offer continuing education or tuition assistance programs. Such programs and their requirements vary considerably. Here are just a few examples:

- An employer may pay an employee's tuition directly to a college.
- An employer may reimburse an employee for tuition the employee has personally paid to a college.
- The assistance may cover only the cost of the tuition itself, or a combination of tuition, books, and fees, or some percentage of eligible expenses.
- There may be a "cap" where the assistance covers up to a certain dollar amount toward eligible expenses, usually on a per-year basis.
- The employer may grant time off work, with pay, to attend college, but not pay for the tuition itself.
- As a condition of participating in the education assistance program, the employer may require the employee to legally commit, in writing, to continue working for the employer for a specified number of years. In the event the

employee leaves the employer or is terminated from employment before the time commitment is met, the student would be required to pay back all or some portion of the assistance provided.
- The employer may hold the employee's accrued vacation or other benefit leave days as collateral to ensure they meet the commitment to remain with the employer a specified length of time.
- In most cases, the employee will be required to maintain a certain minimum grade point average or a minimum passing grade in each course in order to remain eligible for the assistance program.
- Some employers may have limitations as to the course of study which will be allowed. For example, an educational assistance program at a life insurance company might not permit reimbursement for college classes leading to a career as a dental hygienist, whereas pursuit of a business degree would be approved. The rationale, of course, is that training in the dental field is not related to the employer's industry in any way and the company would therefore not benefit. Fortunately, many, if not most, employers support education of their staff regardless of the field of study and have no such restrictions.

SPECIAL STATE PROGRAMS

Some states have launched special programs to assist their citizens in obtaining the education required for higher-paying jobs. These programs frequently offer free college tuition or other types of aid.

Note: Government-sponsored programs come and go, and their continuation usually depends on the availability of federal or state funding. The programs cited here are presented merely as examples and may no longer exist or may have changed their award offerings or eligibility requirements.

One example is the Maryland Community College Promise Scholarship program. This scholarship is a "last-dollar" award that provides tuition assistance for eligible Maryland high school graduates (or equivalent) to attend one of Maryland's public community colleges. A last-dollar scholarship is one that is awarded when all other available financial resources (personal funds, other scholarships, grants, etc.) still fall short of the amount needed to cover tuition and fees.

The New York State Excelsior Scholarship, in combination with other student financial aid programs, allows residents who meet eligibility requirements to attend a SUNY or CUNY college tuition-free.

The COVID-19 pandemic also triggered some new educational support programs. For example, in 2020, the State of Michigan initiated the Futures for Frontliners program to provide educational assistance to essential workers who did not have college degrees. Once that program ended, Michigan Reconnect, a new state program, was introduced in 2021 to offer tuition-free community college to all Michigan residents who are twenty-five or older and do not have a college degree.

Sometimes, problematic costs extend beyond college tuition. Even when those are covered, working parents will often need child care for their small children in order to attend classes. Do not automatically assume you cannot attend college because of the need for child care. Each state receives funds from the federal government for state-run child care subsidy programs. These programs help low-income families pay for child care so they can attend school. Individual colleges may also have child care programs to assist their students.

Be sure to check online to see if your state has any special programs for which you may be eligible. These are also frequently reported on local TV news, and college financial offices will know of them.

IS EVERYONE IN AGREEMENT?

You might think that since you are the one pursuing the required education, you are the only one who needs to approve the idea. Think again. Often, your decision to address this time-consuming readiness factor will directly impact your spouse or significant other, your children, your current employer, and/or other persons or organizations which may be important in your life. You need to make sure those affected by your decisions also support this endeavor.

Since college or training programs can be stressful, challenging, and demanding of your time, I highly recommend you have a serious, sit-down talk with those who might be impacted and ask for their understanding, agreement, patience, and support. Your spouse or significant other will certainly experience more alone time and may need to take on additional chores around the home, watch the kids more, or provide other types of support. You may need to ask your current employer for some flexibility in your hours or work schedule in order to take required courses, some of which may only be offered at inconvenient times.

Since you usually pursue education to secure a better life for both you and your family, you might think everyone would automatically be supportive. Unfortunately, that's not always the case.

A colleague told me about the experience of a college student whom I will call Brian. Brian was in his early twenties and married with two young children. Both he and his wife worked in low-paying jobs, and even with their combined incomes, they could barely make ends meet. Brian decided to pursue a new, higher-paying career. However, to secure a job in the new field, he would first need to complete his bachelor's degree.

While Brian was motivated and up for the challenge, his wife was not, and she protested angrily. Despite her objections, Brian proceeded anyway. In retaliation, she attempted to derail his efforts by throwing down obstacles at every opportunity. For example, she demanded he not spend any time whatsoever studying or doing homework in the evening until she and the children had gone to bed. As a result, after working all day, Brian stayed up late every night studying and then had to drag himself into work early the next morning. Sometimes, out of spite, Brian's wife would go so far as to destroy his class notes or delete his classwork files from their home computer. As you would expect, Brian was miserable and his grades suffered. Unfortunately, no one ever learned what eventually became of Brian, but I suspect things did not end well.

Yes, Brian's story is certainly an extreme case, and there may have been other issues involved. However, the point is that the level of support you might receive from others can range anywhere from total cooperation to active sabotage. Only you know your unique situation and the personalities of the individuals involved. Securing agreement and cooperation from everyone who may play a role can be critical to your success. Don't overlook or underestimate the significance of support!

Believe me, I personally understand many of the challenges associated with the education readiness factor, as I earned two degrees while working full-time and having a family. My wife and I discussed the education plan in advance. She recognized the future value of this effort for our family and was totally supportive. Still, finding a balance of personal life, work, and college was difficult for us both. When I needed to hide away to read, study for exams, or write papers, she graciously took on additional responsibilities around the house and with the kids as needed. It was hard, but as a team, we made it work.

At the end of my undergraduate program, I needed just one more class, a certain required course, to graduate. Unfortunately, it was only offered during the day when I was normally scheduled to work (online classes were not yet available). I discussed the situation with both the college professor and my immediate supervisor at work. The professor was understanding and agreed to work out a solution. He allowed me to work independently and attend class only periodically, mostly to take exams. My employer was supportive and willing to flex my work schedule temporarily as needed. Consulting all the involved parties in advance paid off. Thanks to their cooperation, I was able to complete the required course and graduate on schedule.

I share my story not because I am looking for any kudos for my efforts, but because it is a real-world example of how getting everyone on board with your educational plan is possible—and it can work!

YOUR PERSONAL READINESS: EDUCATION AND TRAINING

- Have you consciously made a personal commitment to dedicate the time and effort needed to complete the required education or training?
- Have you researched the minimum educational requirements for the career you want by reviewing numerous job descriptions and postings?
- Do you know the specific type of education or training you will need?
- If a degree is needed, do you know the specific major or name of the degree?
- Does the college, college curriculum, or non-college training program need to be accredited, and if so, by whom?
- Have you researched all available financial aid, assistance programs, or other resources?

➢ Have you taken steps to ensure the individuals important in your life agree with your decision to move ahead with your education or training?

Experience

You may do a good job of describing your talents, but let's be real—a potential employer just doesn't know you. That is why employers look at previous verifiable work experience as evidence that that a candidate can actually do the job. For them, past performance is considered a predictor of future performance.

Think about the hiring process from the viewpoint of the employer. In most cases, applicants are complete unknowns to the interviewers, and selecting one for hire represents a very real element of risk. Finding a candidate with solid experience helps the hiring parties feel they are minimizing that risk and therefore less apt to make a "bad hire" (i.e., someone who eventually just does not work out). A bad hire represents a significant cost to an organization. Wages are wasted on someone who will eventually quit or be fired, time is lost, and the position is once again unfilled, resulting in still more recruiting costs.

Employers dream of attracting experienced applicants with proven track records of success, who, when hired, can immediately "hit the ground running" with a minimum of training. Such candidates have a smaller learning curve and already made their mistakes somewhere else, while on someone else's payroll.

Dream on, employer. For most employers, receiving applications exclusively from such ideal candidates is usually just that—only a dream. In the real world, candidates tend to fall into one of four categories relating to experience (best-case to worst-case) where they have:

- Exactly the right amount and type of experience sought by the employer.
- The right type of work experience, but not as much as desired by the employer.
- Work experience, but not the specific type sought by the employer.
- Minimal or no relevant work experience.

Regardless of which category you fall into, each of the following sections can help you capitalize on whatever level of experience you already have.

I HAVE THE RIGHT EXPERIENCE

If you fall into this category, great! Your major challenge will be to clearly communicate to the interviewer that you have solid experience and can perform this type of work. I have seen many applicants who appear to have good work experience, but fail to effectively convey that fact on their resumes and cover letters and are unable to articulate it during the interview. Although I might suspect they may be able to do the work, my responsibility as an interviewer is to be sure. Again, the employer does not know you and cannot risk assuming you can "probably" do the job.

As an experienced applicant, your preparation calls for examining which aspects of your work history would be of most interest to the potential employer and then finding ways to communicate it. Doing so effectively helps to eliminate any doubt in the mind of the hiring party. You would be surprised how many applicants describe their work experience in extremely general, vague terms, so much so they tend to confuse the potential employer about what they actually did in their previous or current job.

Imagine the following two candidates describing their respective work experience during an interview:

Candidate 1: *"I worked as a Client Consultant at the ABC Company and sold products. We used Microsoft Office software. I helped with invoices."*

Candidate 2: *"I have been a Client Consultant with the XYZ Company for the past four years. This is a commissioned inside sales position, and I primarily supply National and Motorola custom surface-mount electronic components to the automotive industry. My primary clients are General Motors and Ford. My sales goals are met or exceeded every quarter. I am very proficient with Microsoft Office, especially Word, Excel, and PowerPoint. In fact, others in my department will often come to me for assistance with these applications. Part of my responsibility includes personally working with the client and our accounts receivable department to investigate and resolve any invoice discrepancies."*

While the two candidates in this example are fictitious, I have found that hearing a vague work experience description such as that provided by Candidate 1 is not all that unusual during a job interview. Obviously, Candidate 2 was much clearer and more specific regarding what their work experience entailed. After speaking with Candidate 1, an interviewer may be thinking:

- What the heck does a Client Representative at the ABC Company actually do? That title could mean anything.
- Exactly what products did this person sell?
- Did this person work on a commission basis?
- Was this candidate good at sales?
- Was this an inside or outside sales position?
- How long was the person at the ABC Company? Are they still employed there?
- Who were this individual's customers?
- The ABC Company may have Microsoft Office, but did the candidate use it, and if so, which applications and versions?
- Is the candidate proficient with any of the applications? Nothing was stated which seemed to suggest proficiency.
- The candidate "helped" with invoices, but in what capacity and level of detail, and with what degree of responsibility?

Sure, an experienced and skilled interviewer could ask follow-up questions in an attempt to "pull" this information out of the applicant, but why bother? If a candidate cannot articulate basic facts about their own work experience any better than this, perhaps this person is not the best choice.

Why do so many candidates tend to be vague about their work experience on their applications, resumes, cover letters, and during interviews? Maybe they have not prepared for the interview or given much advance thought as to how that experience should be conveyed to the employer. Perhaps it is because they subscribe to the old and flawed notion that experience on resumes should be presented in a "one-size-fits-all" manner and need not be tailored for each job position they seek. Maybe they feel modifying the resume for each prospective employer would be too much work. Or, they may believe—incorrectly—that if their work experience is presented in a sufficiently vague and generic manner, a potential employer will make assumptions and just mentally and favorably fill in the resulting blanks.

I HAVE WORK EXPERIENCE, BUT NOT THE AMOUNT OR SPECIFIC TYPE SOUGHT

In this case, you have three strategies available:

- Make the most of what experience you already have.

- See what you can do to grow and enhance your experience between now and the next job search.
- Look for opportunities and positions which demand less specific experience up front, but which provide a potential direct path to the desired job.

If you are looking for a job today, the reality is that you have the experience that you have. At the moment, there is not much you can do about it other than to paint it in the most favorable light possible. However, for the next job search—and this is where readiness comes in—you need to actively determine what steps you can take now to add at least some elements of the work sought by the employer into your experience.

When you just don't have the specific experience sought by employers, your approach when pursuing a new position should include:

- Giving examples of experience in your current job that are relevant and would readily transfer to the new line of work.
- Emphasizing that you are successful at your current job, but looking to grow professionally.
- Providing examples of specific situations that demonstrate you are a motivated, able, willing, and fast learner. Having an excellent high school or college grade point average may help illustrate this, along with describing any learning experiences you have undertaken at your current job.
- Conveying any skills or knowledge you do have that are specifically related to the new type of work; however, do not bluff or exaggerate, as the interviewer will find you out in a second.
- Emphasizing any special training or other learning you may have undertaken on your own initiative in preparation for the new type of work.
- Pointing out your passion and interest in pursuing the type of work you are seeking (if all candidates have only limited experience, the one who is "hungry" to grow may be most attractive).

If your lack of specific experience repeatedly prevents you from being able to obtain positions despite your best efforts to spin things favorably, then you need to see what you can do to expand your experience for next time.

The following suggestions will apply differently to everyone depending on the field you are in and the organization for which you work. First, when management is looking for volunteers for a project, sign up. Not only will you acquire additional experience, but you will gain visibility. Similarly, your supervisor may be willing to appoint you to serve on an organization-wide committee or task force. Note that some committees are considered prestigious and wield considerable power in approving budgets, projects, purchases, etc.; especially early on, it is unlikely you would be assigned to one of these. However, another benefit of serving on any organization-wide committee is that you gain exposure to other departments or work areas with which you may not normally have contact. This is beneficial as, in addition to developing an internal professional network, you may discover one of these other areas interests you as a possible new career option.

Second, if your company has a career development program through which employees can gain new skills and experiences in new areas, check it out. Consider looking at "job enhancement," a situation where you use your existing position to learn new skills and types of work. If you are already proficient at your current job and have a good relationship with your supervisor, see whether it would be possible to take on new or additional tasks—not necessarily for extra pay, just for the opportunity to learn these new skills. At this point, you are looking to fatten the experience section of your resume, not your wallet. Supervisors and managers frequently have a large degree of latitude about work assignments—except when higher pay will be involved. While this may sound simple enough, do not be surprised if you still encounter some obstacles.

- Due to laws or for liability reasons, the new type of work may require a license or other credential. For example, a hospital orderly who wants to pursue a career in nursing cannot be legally allowed to pass out medications just to gain such experience.

- Your coworkers may give you some hassle and accuse you of "brown-nosing" the boss or ask if you are trying to make them look bad through your extra efforts. Odds are they will not be sympathetic to your intentions. After all, you are working to get ahead, which means they will be left behind. They may accuse you of thinking you are too good for this type of work. You will just need to deal with it; this is really *their* problem due to insecurity or envy.
- If your organization is heavily unionized, you could encounter strong resistance from the employer, the union, or both. The employer does not want to receive grievances about you working "out of class" or "doing someone else's job," and the union may not look kindly on you voluntarily working beyond the scope of your current job description. Depending on the reasonableness of the union leadership and the labor relations department, you may be able to discuss your intentions with all concerned parties and obtain a one-time, non-precedent-setting agreement permitting this arrangement on a temporary basis. The role of the bargaining unit is to look after the needs of its members and advancing your career is a legitimate need. They may agree, so long as the desired arrangement is not felt to be to the detriment of other union members and it does not establish what they may view as a dangerous precedent. If the union agrees, the employer is much more likely to go along with the idea.

Another opportunity may appear if a job vacancy arises, especially when the need to fill it is immediate and urgent. In such cases, the Human Resources (HR) department may open the position temporarily on a "working out of class" or "interim" basis, just to have someone performing the job until it can be permanently filled. Frequently, the requirements for a temporary position may be somewhat more relaxed than for a permanent replacement, and such a position may be a chance for you to obtain credible experience with the new type of work. When an out-of-class job is established on an official basis, the employer and union (if applicable) will already be in agreement with the arrangement. Also, the temporary position might even involve receiving slightly higher pay, although that is not the real goal of taking such an assignment. Working in an out-of-class position has two additional benefits:

- You get to "test drive" the position, usually on a low-risk basis, to see if you like the job enough to pursue it permanently. Such arrangements often allow the individual to easily return to their old position if desired.
- Your immediate supervisor and others who may be involved in the interview process for the permanent position have the opportunity to see you actually performing the job.

If none of the above approaches are viable options, you may wish to consider applying for an entry-level position in the field of choice and accept the fact you may even need to take a pay cut in the short run to do so. Think beyond the current money and remember this is a long-term strategic move. For example, let's say you have worked five years in your current low-level job and are at the top of the pay scale with no realistic room for growth. If the new job opens the door to a new career path involving the possibility of advancement based on experience, and you would eventually be making considerably more money for years to come, it may be worth the temporary reduction in pay to secure that opportunity. Some may argue moving backward in pay will hurt your resume, but there may be no other option. This is a hard choice you may need to consider.

I HAVE LITTLE OR NO WORK EXPERIENCE

Experience is the readiness factor for which many individuals feel trapped in a "Catch-22" situation. Employers only want applicants with experience, but if no one will hire them, how can they ever get the needed experience? Recent graduates may find themselves in precisely this situation; they may have the required education, but lack the work experience sought by employers. Additionally, competing with more experienced applicants in the job market for the same position can be a daunting challenge. What can an applicant do?

Realistically, your only option is to make the most of what you have. Explain how any work or even non-work related experience you have demonstrates that you would make an excellent, hard-working employee.

- You may not immediately think of it this way, but being a successful server at a restaurant, a retail store clerk, etc. teaches one how to deal with customers, determine and meet their needs, and resolve any problems. These types of jobs are nothing short of customer service boot camps, and previous success in such positions may help demonstrate you at least have experience working with people and a customer service focus and attitude.
- If you did an internship, clinical rotation in a medical field, apprenticeship, or had some other on-the-job training or experience, explain how this benefitted you and will also benefit the potential employer. Employers may not always be willing to count such experiences towards meeting the official "work experience" requirement of the job, but you can check, and regardless, use it to put the best face on what you have.
- Do you volunteer in some capacity at your church, a club, or are you significantly involved with a community project or organization? Perhaps you write and edit the church bulletin, serve as a scout leader, help deliver "meals on wheels" to the elderly, schedule and lead work teams for a community cleanup project, or do all the promotional photography for a charitable organization. It might be a bit of a stretch, but if these examples prove you have specific, desirable skills and have already performed certain types of work—even for free—you are still ahead of other applicants who may have no such experience to show. Additionally, some organizations value having their employees involved in community service activities; if so, this could work in your favor.

YOUR PERSONAL READINESS: EXPERIENCE

➤ Have you prepared all written materials and applications so they clearly detail the important aspects of your experience?

➤ Are you able to clearly and concisely articulate relevant aspects of your experience if asked during an interview?

➤ Have you investigated numerous open positions and job descriptions in the field you wish to pursue, to learn the level and type of experience employers are seeking in the market today?

➤ Have you explored job enhancement, training, working out-of-class, or other such opportunities for experience with your current employer?

➤ Have you considered whether attaining your ultimate career goals may involve changing to a different job, perhaps even accepting an entry-level position just to obtain the experience needed?

Skills (and Abilities)

Most people would probably agree education and training do not necessarily translate into guaranteed skill. I once had a summer job working in a hospital as a phlebotomist. A phlebotomist is a person whose duties include drawing blood from you when your physician orders lab tests.

My training involved being told how the procedure works and becoming familiar with the equipment used (different size needles, the various colored tubes, tube holder, tourniquet, etc.). Next, I shadowed an experienced phlebotomist, observing the technique and order in which the steps were performed. These steps included patient verification and identification, selecting the correct colored tube for the ordered test, tube labeling, how and where the tourniquet was applied, locating an accessible vein, etc. In between the observation trips, I practiced my technique by repeatedly inserting a needle into a stretched rubber tube taped to a tabletop. Finally, two very brave phlebotomists volunteered to let me draw a vial or two of their blood to see how well I had learned everything.

Okay, are you ready to be my next patient? If you are hesitant and squirming a bit, why? You are likely thinking that although I may know *how* to draw blood, I probably do not yet have enough experience to be *proficient* at it. Most likely, you would prefer I obtain that experience by first drawing blood from someone other than you! Think about it. What if an interviewer has any doubts about a candidate's skill level? They would likely think the person should gain experience elsewhere, making the usual beginner mistakes while on someone else's payroll!

Consider a new IT (information technology) technician working on a complex computer network installation. Although the technician may be educated on how a network should be configured or wired, their actual technical skill level may still be weak due to having only a limited amount of practical, hands-on experience. These skills might involve setting network parameters in the software, physically running cables back to the router closet, reading wiring diagrams, and correctly terminating the wires.

Until the technician has acquired adequate experience and sufficiently developed the needed skills, the individual may unintentionally cause some installation problems requiring rework or troubleshooting by a more seasoned employee. A new and somewhat inexperienced technician would probably not be assigned sole responsibility for a new installation at the site of an important and valuable client, but might instead assist under the guidance of a skilled individual while developing the needed skill sets.

Employers know the difference between receiving education and training and actually possessing the needed skills. Although they expect you to have gained some skills during the education and training, they know it is not guaranteed, and any skills you have acquired thus far may not be fully developed. Given this, potential employers often look to your work experience as surrogate evidence of your skill. If you did the job acceptably for your current or a previous employer, the assumption is that you likely have the skill. Even then, employers may still be nervous about hiring you as they are relying on indirect and external evidence of your skill level. They have not had the reassurance of seeing your competency with their own eyes. For this reason, it is not uncommon for interview sessions to sometimes include an exercise where you are asked to demonstrate a particular skill set.

For example, I know an organization that routinely hires data analysts. As part of the interview process, candidates are taken to a quiet conference room and given a laptop computer (no internet access) loaded with Microsoft Excel, a set of data, and a list of questions regarding the data. During a one-hour time period, the candidate is expected to use Excel to analyze the data and then answer the questions based on the analysis. All resulting work, tables, graphs, formulas, and so forth are to be saved in an Excel file for later review by the interviewers. To get to this point in the hiring process, each applicant has claimed on their application materials to be proficient in Excel and to already have direct work experience using Excel to analyze data. Since each candidate has the required education, training, and work experience, this exercise should be a no-brainer, right?

Unfortunately, this employer found that was not the case. Some applicants completely botched the exercise, either by giving erroneous answers or, in some cases, no answers at all. Yes, some applicants actually sat looking at the computer screen for the entire hour with no clue how to proceed. This is very interesting, as their applications, resumes, and cover letters all clearly stated they had the requisite education, training, skill, and experience needed for such a task. Yet, many obviously could not perform the task.

When you view the skills readiness factor through the eyes of a potential employer, it becomes apparent your challenge as an applicant is to:

- Identify which specific skills are sought by the employer.
- Be ready to demonstrate that you have those skills.

Of course, the above assumes you actually possess the necessary skills. If you do not, or if they are weak, then the challenge additionally involves developing or enhancing those skills to a sufficient level.

As a readiness factor, your skills need to include the following:

- Job-specific skills
- Communication (verbal and presentation)
- Communication (written)
- Interpersonal skills
- Physical abilities
- Leadership skills

JOB-SPECIFIC SKILLS

The types of job-specific skills sought by potential employers are so varied and numerous they cannot all be addressed here. However, valuable information may be readily found in job postings for the career you wish to pursue. Every job description lists the skills which the employer has indicated are required or desirable for the position. Once you have identified these skills, your task is to:

- Decide which of the skills are most applicable and attainable for your situation.
- Rate yourself—honestly—on your current proficiency level with these skills.
- Make a to-do list for acquiring or developing any skills which are currently missing or need improvement.
- Systematically carry out the to-do list.

COMMUNICATION AND INTERPERSONAL SKILLS

Every individual needs communication and interpersonal skills to succeed in any career field, or for that matter, to successfully pass a job interview. However, the expected proficiency level for these skills will vary depending on the position. For example, an applicant for a sales representative position would naturally be expected to have a much higher communication and interpersonal skill level than someone applying for a job as a machine operator or worker on an assembly line.

The need for verbal and presentation skills may arise even if your position does not typically call for them daily. For example, a civil engineer working for a county road commission may need to periodically speak at public hearings or information forums, testify in court as a witness, appear on camera with a news reporter about a new road project, or be involved in similar situations. Public speaking was probably not a required course in engineering school, but even if you have taken such a class, you already know that education alone does not necessarily equal skill.

Most people dread the thought of public speaking. You will even see statistics rating the fear of public speaking (known as glossophobia) above the fear of death. I have always wondered about the validity of statistics that rate the fear of public speaking so high, and perhaps you questioned them as well. My assumption was that, although people may try to avoid public speaking at all costs, even if it negatively impacts their careers, they would do so when there is just no other choice. However, to fear public speaking more than death always seemed somewhat extreme. As it turns out, I had a chance to witness firsthand how terrified some people can be at the prospect of speaking to a group.

As a requirement for an undergraduate program, I had to take a business communication course which included public speaking. In this class, which only had about twelve students, every student was occasionally required to go to the podium and speak for five minutes on any topic. One student, a middle-aged woman, absolutely panicked when she learned about this requirement on the first day of class. She insisted it was just not possible for her to do this. However, the instructor informed her that it would need to become possible if she wished to pass, and this was a required course for graduation!

The first time the student attempted to speak at the podium, she froze and burst into tears within seconds, then promptly retreated to her seat, crying. At each session, the instructor tried to reassure the student by reminding her that we were a friendly audience. The student personally knew most of her fellow classmates, and she should think of the presentation as just speaking with friends. Still, there was just something about standing behind that podium that struck terror in her, so much so she could not even function.

The good news is that with each effort to speak, her self-confidence slowly grew and the student held it together longer each time. By the end of the course, she was able to speak for the entire required time. Her presentation skills may not have been great, but they were sufficient to the point where, although she looked nervous, she was functional and not panicked. The first time she completed her presentation successfully, everyone applauded and complimented her as she returned to her seat. She smiled and beamed with satisfaction at having overcome this personal phobia and challenge. After that, I had a much deeper appreciation of just how real and debilitating the fear of public speaking can be for some individuals.

If your ability to verbally communicate effectively and confidently could use some improvement, explore the resources which may be available in your area. One low-cost and informal resource about which I have heard generally favorable reviews is Toastmasters. Most local chapters of the organization will let you attend a meeting at no cost to see what it is all about. Other options, although these would involve expense, include taking a course at a local college or attending a public speaking seminar from organizations such as Dale Carnegie. I mention these organizations not as endorsements, but simply as potential resources to further investigate.

Public speaking aside, the need for good verbal, written, and interpersonal communication skills should be obvious. Realistically, everyone in the working world has to communicate with someone, be it their boss, coworkers, vendors, or customers, and are expected to do so in an intelligent manner. Initially, one may think that written communication skills are of minimal importance for many jobs, but I disagree. While your job description or duties may not routinely involve writing, correspondence, advertising copy, detailed reports, or other such materials, there is a greater need for writing skills than you might realize. Consider the following:

- Anyone providing any type of service typically must write a work summary or something similar on a customer's invoice or job ticket.
- A worker in almost any field may need to someday fill out an on-the-job incident or accident report, providing a written, detailed account of what occurred. What you write and how it is written might potentially have legal ramifications, both for you and the organization.
- Unless you completely control the budget and purse strings at your workplace, at some point you will likely need to write a justification or proposal for a new idea or equipment acquisition, which will then be sent "up the food chain" for review and approval.

- If you are or become a supervisor in a unionized workplace (or you are a union steward), you will need to provide written responses to grievances. Like proposals, these frequently go up the chain of command and could end up at arbitration hearings. How effectively you write your statements may help determine the outcome.
- Regular communication with your supervisor or coworkers may be in a written format via email, text, or other message application.

The above list could go on and on. Imagine what a customer would think when the high-dollar repair invoice they just received contains numerous misspelled words and grammatical errors: *I hope their technical skills are better than how they write!* Even if you don't deal with customers directly, per se, imagine the impression you leave on others with poorly written communication. If you submit a budget request or proposal which contains incoherent sentences and grammatical errors, what confidence will others have in your ideas? Many times, the audience for your written material will be individuals from elsewhere in the organization who do not personally know you, and how you write will create their first and only impression of you. Whether fair or not, *how you communicate in writing reflects directly on you.* To be blunt, if your report, proposal, or other document reads like it was written by an incompetent fool, it will be assumed you are one.

Based on my experience and observations in management over many years, I always give the following advice to students in my college classes and to employees who are looking to advance their careers:

The writing skills of most people today are generally so poor that all you have to do is write reasonably well and you will be noticed.

Notice the words "reasonably well." You do not have to be the next Ernest Hemingway or J.K. Rowling of your workplace.

PHYSICAL ABILITIES

Some fields, especially law enforcement and firefighting, usually require applicants to possess a certain level of physical fitness and ability. Candidates for such positions may be required to perform a series of specific tasks before or during the recruitment or interview process. These tasks might involve doing a certain number of exercises (e.g., sit-ups, push-ups, running stairs, etc.), completing a series of timed tasks (e.g., being able to carry or drag a certain amount of weight, run an obstacle course, etc.), and so forth.

Requiring certain physical abilities to enter these careers is not and cannot be an arbitrary demand, but must be a legitimate prerequisite based on the routine physical expectations of the job. For example, a police officer may very well need to chase a suspect on foot for two blocks and jump fences to ultimately apprehend the offender. A firefighter may need to pick up and carry an unconscious 150-pound victim down a ladder to save their life. Clearly, candidates who lack these abilities would be unable to satisfactorily perform the job and are therefore unable to ensure the safety of the public or themselves.

Human resources professionals refer to a skill or other requirement legitimately mandated for a position as a *Bona Fide Occupational Qualification* (BFOQ). Companies may run into legal problems if they arbitrarily require a skill for a position and that mandated skill is not a BFOQ. For example, requiring applicants for an office accounting position to demonstrate that they can lift and carry 100 pounds up a twenty-foot ladder would make no sense whatsoever. When the physical requirements for a job do not legitimately match the usual demands and expectations of that position, discrimination claims may arise. For example, courts have determined that, in some cases, rigorous physical requirements were deliberately established by employers for the purpose of discriminating against women.

On the other hand, consider a traveling sales representative for an industrial equipment firm who must routinely, without help, transport and show bulky and heavy devices to customers or set up such items at trade shows. The description for this position might legitimately include a requirement such as "the ability to move, carry, and lift equipment weighing up to 60 pounds" if the job routinely involves handling items of that weight.

Again, the physical skills expected for positions where they are a BFOQ should be found in the job description itself or on the employer's website in a section describing the recruitment and hiring process. For example, to minimize its length and complexity, a job description may simply state that an applicant must "possess the physical abilities determined to be necessary for the position." Elsewhere, applicants would find detailed information regarding the specific physical skills and abilities expected and to be tested.

Obviously, if certain physical skills and abilities are necessary for your career field, your readiness will also involve determining whether you already can or will be able to meet these requirements.

LEADERSHIP SKILLS

Individuals with supervisory or management career goals, as well as those seeking self-employment as the owner of a company, need to consider leadership skills. Are leaders born or created? This is an age-old debate among experts which will certainly not be definitively resolved here.

Consider this: You may know individuals who are excellent artists or musicians but never had a teacher or even a single class. These gifted individuals seem to have been born with incredible natural talent. Others, born without such inherent abilities, typically must work hard and struggle through art or music instruction to gain a respectable level of skill. So, are artists and musicians born or created? As training and experience will help anyone develop and improve whatever baseline level of skills they may already possess, the answer may be a little of both.

The average person cannot become an accomplished pianist simply by reading a book on the subject. Book knowledge in the brain does not automatically translate into hand dexterity and ability on the keys. Proficiency requires practice and experience over time to build the necessary skills. Such is the case with leadership. True, some individuals are, in fact, natural-born leaders. Others, however, must acquire leadership skills through experience. Where do you rate?

Anyone can give orders. A supervisor may have the authority to say, "Do this or you will be fired!" However, this approach does not constitute leadership. People willingly carry out the directives of a leader not out of fear of punishment, but because they trust and have confidence in the leader.

Leadership ability involves both inward and outward aspects. When examining your own leadership potential, here are a few items to consider:

- Are you personally competent in the subject area you will lead? Individuals will not respect or follow leaders whose own competency is questionable. If your competency is less than optimal, improvement will be a top priority for you.
- Are you professional in your conduct, punctual, and do you meet deadlines, always follow through on promises, and "walk the walk" rather than just talk a good line? Is your temperament consistent and not subject to mood swings? If you cannot honestly answer "yes" to all the above, you must make changes where necessary.
- Those who report to you must see for themselves that you lead by example and are self-disciplined, always exhibiting the above qualities.
- Do you accept responsibility for the decisions you make? If you are wrong or make a mistake, do you admit it? Nobody wants to be blamed for a poor decision made by the leader.
- Are you completely clear when giving instructions to others? Allowing those you lead some flexibility in how to complete a task is often fine, and at times, even desirable. However, if you have specific expectations, these must be communicated. You cannot merely assume others automatically know what you want. Following a leader's vague or unclear directions and then being chastised for the results is demoralizing.

The military is famous and well-respected for its ability to train and develop effective leaders. If you served in the military, you may have already acquired leadership skills that will serve you well in the civilian workplace. However, what if you do not currently have any leadership experience? How can you obtain the experience necessary to develop leadership skills? Here are a few suggestions:

- Volunteer at your present job for assignments or projects which involve leading a team. Management often has difficulty in recruiting volunteers to lead group tasks and will usually welcome someone who willingly steps forward. In addition to gaining leadership experience, your potential for future promotion may be recognized by management.
- If you belong to a club, civic group, or church, these organizations frequently need volunteers to fill board positions. Serving as a president, vice-president, secretary, treasurer, or other such position may offer a relatively low-risk opportunity to gain leadership experience.

YOUR PERSONAL READINESS: SKILLS AND ABILITIES

- ➢ Have you researched and identified the job-specific skills employers require or desire within your particular field by reviewing the job description of current postings by several different employers?
- ➢ Have you honestly and critically evaluated your current proficiency level with those job-specific skills?
- ➢ Do you have a plan as to how you will acquire or further develop those skills?
- ➢ Have you honestly evaluated your communication and interpersonal skills? Do they need improvement? If so, how will you improve them?
- ➢ Does the position have any physical ability requirements? If so, are they attainable for you, and are you working towards readiness?
- ➢ Do your career goals require leadership skills? If so, do you already have such skills or need to acquire them?

Credentials

To work or advance in some career fields, it may not be enough to merely possess the necessary education and skills. You may also need specific credentials. One might argue the word "credentials" itself could apply to an individual's education, training, and work experience, and that would usually be correct. However, that is not the context in which the term is used here when discussing credentials as a readiness factor.

As used here, the term "credential" refers to *verification by an applicable external and recognized entity of one's competency and/or having met a defined set of qualifications (e.g., education, training, experience, etc.) in a specific field*. Credentials may be divided into two main categories: licenses and certifications.

- A *license* is a legally-recognized, formal authorization granted by a government entity permitting one to engage in a specific profession, business, trade, or other such activity. This is not to be confused with a general "business license or permit" issued by local governments primarily for the purposes of code and zoning compliance, safety, and tax collection.
- A *certification*, as the term is used here, refers to a formal endorsement or recognition by a reputable and recognized entity attesting that one has met certain criteria, such as predefined combinations of education, training, experience, acceptance of established ethical standards, etc. Certification, as you will see, might be more correctly known by other various designations that may be applicable to specific fields.

CAVEAT: The licensing and certification information contained herein, including organization names, credential designations, and other information, is presented as a limited list of examples for illustrative purposes only. Many other credentialing entities may exist in any one field. Inclusion of a particular accrediting organization does not constitute an endorsement, and omission of any organization should not be interpreted negatively. Certification and licensing requirements, as well as applicable credentialing organizations, may change without notice. Always check to ensure you rely upon the latest information by consulting the licensing and/or certifying entity for your field.

LICENSING

Why do some jobs require a license, while others of apparent equal or greater importance require only a certification, or perhaps even no credential at all? Here is a real-world example from the medical field regarding medical equipment maintenance and repair. Individuals working in this field are usually employed by hospitals or medical equipment companies and are often known as "biomedical equipment technicians" (BMETs). These skilled technicians calibrate, maintain, and repair electronic and mechanical medical equipment such as heart monitors, defibrillators, IV infusion pumps, and hundreds of other types of medical devices. Obviously, this is important work with potential life-and-death consequences if the work is done improperly.

Some time ago, several technicians attempted to enhance recognition for the field—and possibly receive higher wages, of course—by exploring how to have their state create and require a license for individuals performing such work. The argument went like this: "There are no license requirements for individuals who calibrate and repair life-support medical equipment in hospitals, yet just try and charge someone for a haircut in this state without a barber's license and see what happens!"

On the surface, the argument might sound quite compelling. Does it seem logical that it is illegal to charge for a haircut without a license, but anyone is permitted to disassemble and repair a life-saving heart defibrillator or other such equipment? The technicians received a response from the state explaining that licensing for BMETs is not and would likely never be required, along with the rationale as to why that was the case. States issue licenses to *protect the general public* by ensuring individuals engaged in certain activities meet some type of minimum standards. For example, citizens purchase and receive haircuts directly from a barber or hairdresser. Citizens may purchase construction, remodeling, and repair services directly from contractors, electricians, plumbers, and so forth. Patients may purchase and receive medical services directly from physicians and nurses.

Note that all the above examples have one important common factor: the recipients may usually, but not always, obtain the desired services directly from the provider. This is important, as barbers and hairdressers who do not follow sanitation and safety requirements can expose their clients to health hazards or other dangers. Unqualified contractors might perform work failing to meet building codes, which could result in building collapse, electric shock or fires, mixing of sewage and drinking water, or other potentially lethal hazards for citizens. By the nature of their work, physicians and nurses could endanger the general public in countless, potentially fatal ways.

Therefore, to ensure public safety, the state assumes the role of protector by regulating certain activities and requiring those engaged in providing those specific services to obtain a state-issued license. Does this approach guarantee no citizen will ever suffer or die at the hands of an incompetent service provider? No, of course not, but without any licensing requirements, anyone could perform any service they wish without meeting any minimum standards of training, safety, or competency.

Despite the need to protect the public, licensing is not without its costs and practical limitations. A state which over-regulates business will likely see an exodus of service providers and citizens alike. Operating a state licensing agency represents a sizable cost to taxpayers, usually at the expense of other state programs. Plus, adding regulations is typically not a top priority for lawmakers.

Realistically, not every service provided directly to citizens requires the protection of licensing. Suppose you need a portrait or wedding pictures. You can judge the skill level of the photographer by reviewing their portfolio. Additionally, you may wish to consider the recommendations of others. If you plan to have your living room painted, you can check out references and decide whether the resulting work meets your expectations. In these examples, you make your own decision regarding the competency of the service provider. While there may be a risk of dissatisfaction with the resulting product or service, and you may feel you wasted your money, it is unlikely anyone will be injured or die as a result of making a poor choice.

At the other extreme, if no licenses were required, how would you personally assess the competency and clinical skill level of someone who hangs out a sign and claims to be a surgeon? Here, licensure becomes a valuable protective tool.

Returning to the original issue of the BMETs, if no license is required, how does a state protect its citizens from being injured or killed by incompetent medical equipment technicians? Simple: Since such services are rarely sold directly to the general public, the responsibility and burden of ensuring only qualified and competent individuals perform this work is put back onto a licensed entity hiring such service providers. In this case, the technicians were employed by a hospital. A hospital is licensed by the state, and therefore the hospital is responsible for ensuring patient safety by hiring only qualified individuals. Having the state enact laws mandating licensing of BMETs would likely be considered unnecessary overregulation and duplication of effort. The consequences would be higher taxpayer costs incurred by the state to administer and regulate this field and increased costs to hospitals to hire technicians who would likely receive higher wages due to the licensing requirement. Higher costs without any corresponding increase in citizen safety do not make for sound public policy.

As an aside, to put your mind to ease regarding the repair of medical equipment, you will be pleased to know there is a national, formal, and highly-recognized certification process available to BMETs and other professionals working in the field of healthcare technology management. Hospitals, medical equipment companies, and even the military frequently require certification or offer pay incentives to staff who become certified. Certification, which is different from licensing, will be discussed later in this chapter.

DO I NEED A LICENSE?

Despite the responsibility to provide safety to the public, the government does not regulate all businesses, professions, trades, or services to the same extent or in the same way. Some fields may have federal licensing requirements applicable in every state. Others may have licensing requirements that vary considerably by state or local jurisdiction. Still others may not require a license at all. For example, an automobile mechanic who fails to properly install or adjust brakes could potentially kill someone; however, as of this writing, not every state requires licensing of auto mechanics.

If there is no federal licensing mandate, the requirement for a license within a particular line of work depends on the applicable regulations in your state and/or local area. *Always check with applicable regulatory agencies to see if a license is required for your career field.* This can be of real significance when planning to move elsewhere, especially from one state to another. If you plan to relocate, you must thoroughly research the new location's licensing requirements in advance. For example, suppose an auto mechanic intends to move from a state with no licensing requirements to one where each type of automotive work (brakes, emissions systems, etc.) must be individually licensed. If the mechanic does not check this out before moving, they could be in for a big surprise and end up unemployed.

Additionally, some fields, but by no means all, may have *reciprocity agreements* whereby a license granted in one state is recognized in some way by another state. The amount of recognition, if any, may vary considerably. The individual may be allowed a specific time frame in which to obtain a license from the new state of residency, or possession of the old license may be applied in some way toward meeting the requirements for a new license. If you're planning to move and your field requires a license, see if any reciprocity provisions exist.

CERTIFICATION

Certification, which is a verification by an independent, recognized entity that one has met certain criteria, is known by many names and consists of designations specific to the particular field. Sometimes the word "certification" itself is the correct and proper term, but many other terms, titles, and designations exist. Also, certification is usually considered voluntary in nature, but later you will see that in practice this may not always be the case.

For example, consider the certification process for the biomedical equipment technicians mentioned earlier. To become certified, a technician must possess a combination of education and work experience and pass a rigorous written examination. Once a technician has successfully completed all the requirements for certification as defined by the AAMI Credentials Institute (ACI), they are awarded the title of "Certified Biomedical Equipment Technician" (CBET). Certified individuals may then place the CBET initials after their name on business cards, in correspondence, etc.

The above is but one example where the specific term "certified" is used. Many other terms for certification exist within various fields and may instead use designations including:

- Registered
- Specialist
- Professional
- Accredited
- Chartered
- Fellow

Here are just a few examples of certifications and the various credential names applicable to their respective fields and industries:

- In the field of radiology, technicians who are certified by the American Registry of Radiologic Technologists (ARRT) are referred to as "registered" and may use the credential of Registered Technologist (R.T.).

- In the safety management field, individuals who provide professional emergency management services may be certified by the National Association of Safety Professionals (NASP) and are designated as an Emergency Management Specialist (SEM).
- Individuals who provide human resources services may be certified by the Human Resources Certification Institute and receive the designation Professional in Human Resources (PHR).
- Professionals involved in project management may be certified by the Project Management Institute and receive the Project Management Professional (PMP) designation.
- Individuals in the profession of determining the value of properties, which might include gems, jewelry, antiques, artwork, and many other such items, may be certified by the American Society of Appraisers (ASA). One such ASA designation is Accredited Senior Appraiser (ASA).
- Hospital and healthcare management professionals can become a "Fellow" of the American College of Healthcare Executives (ACHE) and receive the FACHE designation.

Who are these certification bodies, and what are their certification requirements? In general, certification is defined and awarded by a reputable and industry-specific organization. Such organizations are typically those widely recognized and accepted as authorities in their respective fields. Requirements for certification vary considerably by profession but typically include some combination of:

- Formal education and training
- Work experience
- Competency verification
- Acceptance of and agreement to adhere to ethical standards or codes of conduct
- Professional references who will attest to the applicant's good character
- Completion of a project
- Community service
- Continuing education (for certification renewal)

Some certification processes may include provisions to make allowances for or even issue a designation to individuals who have entered the certification process in good faith and met some, but not all, of the requirements. An example might be an individual who has taken and passed the required written test but has not yet fulfilled the entire work experience time requirement. Depending on the organization, such an individual may receive a "candidate" designation or a similar title. While usually not considered professional designations, per se, they help potential employers differentiate between those applicants actively working towards certification and those who may have met some of the prerequisites but are not formally pursuing certification.

Competency verification for many certifications consists of a lengthy and challenging written examination. Exam length might run anywhere from an hour up to six or eight hours. While many certification tests are multiple-choice in format, some exams may contain essay questions. Some exams may even require the applicant to give oral responses to a panel of judges. Examinations frequently consist of multiple sections, each covering a different topic or area of focus (e.g., laws and regulations, safety, technical, ethics, etc.). To pass an examination, the applicant must successfully attain a minimum passing score defined by the certifying organization. Additionally, a specified minimum score may be required for each individual section of the exam to receive an overall passing score.

Resources are often available to assist individuals in preparing for certification exams. These include study guides, online practice exams, webinars, or even classroom workshops. Some resources are produced directly by the certifying entity; others may be prepared by various organizations or independent authors. Since most preparatory tools come at a cost to the applicant (and some may be quite expensive), carefully examine the quality. Check with individuals who have already taken the certification exam or read online reviews of the study materials to see if others thought a particular resource was helpful and worth the time and cost.

When planning for a certification examination, you should be aware that certifying organizations often schedule examinations far in advance in a limited number of cities. It is not uncommon for test sites to fill their seats quickly and become closed to additional applicants. Therefore, you should plan your study efforts accordingly, apply early, and allow for an adequate number of months of preparation in advance of the scheduled exam. Some certifying organizations may administer exams themselves, while others may contract with a professional testing service. Such services may have designated test centers or set up temporary locations (such as in hotels) to help accommodate applicants from a wide geographic area. For candidates with disabilities, testing accommodations are typically available, if needed. Some exams may also be available in more than one language or in Braille.

In some cases, you may need to make travel arrangements to get to a test location. To ensure you are rested and prepared for the exam, I recommend you arrive the night before and stay in a nearby hotel so you can do any last-minute studying and get adequate sleep. You are unlikely to do your best if you arrive late and are under stress due to traffic or unfamiliarity with the location. Some test sites do not admit you after the examination begins, regardless of the excuse.

Immediately after completing the exam, take a well-deserved break. Then, while everything is still fresh, write down everything you can recall about the test, especially any material you found difficult. If, unfortunately, you do not pass the written exam on the first try, having detailed notes about the challenging questions and subject areas will aid you greatly in preparing for the next attempt.

YOU MIGHT NEED BOTH

Thus far, licenses and certifications have been discussed as the separate credentials they are. However, in some circumstances, the two go hand-in-hand, and your career field may call for both.

Think about the challenge a state legislature or agency encounters when implementing a licensing requirement for a particular occupation. The state takes on the task and expense of developing, writing, and administering an examination covering the applicable subject material. This task would likely need to be outsourced at a considerable cost as the state agency may not have a qualified subject matter expert on staff. As a solution, the state may consider an alternative and far more cost-effective approach. Suppose a widely-recognized and highly reputable certifying body already exists in a particular field. If so, the state could simply mandate the attainment of that organization's industry-recognized certification credential as a prerequisite for issuing a state license. Why should the state spend taxpayer money to reinvent the wheel?

An example of this potential dual requirement may be found in the area of automotive technology. A well-known certifying entity for automobile service technicians is the National Institute for Automotive Service Excellence (ASE). The ASE is an independent, nonprofit organization working to "improve the quality of vehicle repair and service by testing and certifying automotive professionals." Mechanics may receive certification in general areas such as "Auto Maintenance and Light Repair" or attain certification in any number of very specialized areas of expertise, such as "Damage Analysis & Estimating" or "Advanced Engine Performance."

Depending on where (state/locality) and with whom an automotive technician seeks employment, they may find that:

- No licensing or certification requirements exist at all.
- Although perhaps not required, it may be desirable to have one or more ASE certifications as part of your resume. Having certifications may help favorably differentiate you from the other applicants who do not have any at all.
- The potential employer may require applicants to have one or more ASE certifications in order to be considered for employment.
- State law may require automotive technicians to have ASE certifications to perform automotive repair services in that state.
- A state may also issue its own license for individuals performing automotive services in that state. Proof of one or more ASE certifications may be a requirement to be eligible for licensure.
- Some localities (city, county, etc.) may have their own requirements.

As you can see in some cases, possession of a certification may be a precondition for eligibility to receive a state license. In that situation, both a license and certification are required. When that is the case, the "voluntary" certification is suddenly not-so-voluntary, and without the certification, one cannot obtain the required state license and find employment. When considering employment in a field that may involve both, be sure to carefully check what relationship, if any, exists between these credentials.

OBTAINING A CREDENTIAL AS A CONDITION OF EMPLOYMENT

So long as there is no legal prohibition for doing so, some employers may be willing to hire a candidate for a position that calls for a credential, even if the individual does not possess it at the time of employment. In these cases, employers will usually require the new hire to obtain the particular credential by a specified date as a condition of continued employment. As an example, see the excerpt below from an actual job posting for a hospital laboratory medical technologist.

> Credentials:
> - Bachelor's degree in laboratory science or medical technology from an accredited college/university with MT (ASCP) or MLS (ASCP) CM certification within 1 year of hire.

The good news is that by delaying the credential requirement for a year, the posting may attract more applicants, a plus for the employer. For the applicant, it makes the credential readiness factor less critical, at least in the short run. The downside to this conditional arrangement is that, should the new hire fail to obtain the required credential within the specified time frame, their employment would be terminated.

This arrangement might sound quite risky, but consider the following: Taking a job in the field and working full-time might actually enhance one's ability to pass a credentialing examination. The hands-on experience and knowledge gained through employment could help turn abstract textbook knowledge into practical, in-depth knowledge. Certainly, anyone considering conditional employment with such a requirement needs to know their own state of readiness and the likelihood they can successfully obtain the credentials during the allowed time frame.

As you might suspect, positions requiring a credential almost always make maintenance of that credential a requirement throughout the term of employment, at least for that specific position. In such cases, the employee will be required to periodically prove the credential has been renewed and is still in effect, usually by submitting a copy or other proof. In some cases, verification of credential renewal may be accessible online. Responsibility for keeping a credential current typically falls solely on the employee; it is, after all, the employee's credential. Although the employer may track the expiration date, do not expect your employer to remind you to renew!

Some employers may identify items as simple as a regular driver's license as a job-required credential, even when the position may primarily involve desk or office work. I recall a situation where an employee's driver's license had been revoked due to numerous traffic violations. When the employer discovered the individual no longer had a valid license, the employee was immediately fired for failure to maintain a required credential.

YOUR PERSONAL READINESS: CREDENTIALS

> ➢ Have you researched the credentials deemed desirable, expected, or required by employers for your specific field by reviewing numerous job postings?
> ➢ Have you researched the license and/or certification required by law (if any) for your state and locality?
> ➢ Have you researched the recognized organizations that issue certifications in your field?
> ➢ Do you know the various requirements which must be met to attain certification or licensure?

Credentials

- Are you eligible to pursue certification or licensure at this time?
- Are you prepared to invest the time, expense, and effort required to obtain the necessary credentials?

Differentiation

You now know that employers often view the selection and hiring process as risky. Hiring the wrong individual fails to secure the needed human resource and results in extra work and stress for everyone, especially when the new employee cannot adequately perform the job and must ultimately be terminated.

As mentioned in the overview chapter, when interviewers look at their job candidates, they feel as if they are looking at a group of unknown, clone-like individuals who all have:

- The same required degree
- Nicely prepared resumes and cover letters
- Similar work experience and references
- Any required license, certification, or other credentials
- Dressed nicely and appropriately
- Good interpersonal skills, and are polite and well-spoken

How can an employer minimize the risk of a bad hire and select the best applicant, especially when there is no clear-cut way to tell the candidates apart? As the job applicant, you may feel prepared and confident because you meet all the requirements and have everything needed (degree, resume, credentials, etc.). However, given that the other candidates also meet these requirements, what makes you think you are anything special? How do you convince the interviewers *you* are the best choice? In the marketing field, the solution to this dilemma is known as *differentiation*. Let's see how it works.

PASS A TISSUE, PLEASE

Suppose you urgently need to wipe your nose and ask someone for a tissue. Do you really care which brand they have handy? You just need a tissue. For many people, a tissue is a tissue. When shopping, they may purchase whatever brand of tissue the store happens to carry, whichever one is less expensive or on sale, all without giving the decision much deliberate thought.

However, for tissue companies, this situation is an absolute nightmare! How do they convince you, the consumer, to always select their brand over the competition? Not only do they want your repeat business, but if forced to compete on price alone, profit margins will be lower for everyone in the tissue business.

The goal of marketing differentiation is to convince the buyer that a specific product or service is so favorably different from the offerings of all the other competitors that it is the only clear and logical choice. Putting price aside (sellers rarely prefer to compete on price alone!), how can tissue manufacturers advertise or in some other way present their own tissue such that consumers will believe it is significantly different from other tissues and faithfully purchase only their brand? Here are a few approaches manufacturers may use to differentiate their facial tissue:

- Advertise more frequently so consumers will immediately recognize the brand name and associate it with tissues.
- Place the product in a favorable position on store shelves.
- Ensure availability in as many different stores and store chains as possible.
- Advertise the tissue as being softer than other brands and therefore gentler on the nose.

- Emphasize the tissue as being both stronger and more absorbent than competing tissues.
- Provide the customer with a choice between unscented and scented.
- Offer the option for tissues to contain aloe or similar soothing substances.
- Present a choice of tissue colors.
- Stress how the product has more tissues per box than other brands (even though the actual cost per tissue may be higher!).
- Make the boxes attractive in appearance.
- Offer different sizes and shapes of boxes.

Who knew selling a box of tissues could be so involved and complicated? Here's the payoff for all the effort: If the customer can be successfully convinced that one or more of the above attributes makes a particular tissue superior and more desirable, then the differentiation effort has worked. In the future, the consumer will likely develop the habit of faithfully purchasing only that brand. When that happens, product price may not even be a consideration.

Returning to careers, the "buyer" is the interviewer, and you are the "product" being offered. The critical question is: *What do you offer that the other candidates do not, making you clearly the best choice?*

HOW CAN I DIFFERENTIATE MYSELF?

To differentiate yourself from the other candidates, you will need to move beyond having only the minimum, expected requirements (degree, resume, credentials, etc.). After all, every other candidate possesses these as well. In fact, some applicants may even have a slight advantage over you in some way. Perhaps they attended a more prestigious college or worked for a more impressive organization than the one shown on your resume.

The suggestions below are not necessarily quick, easy, or inexpensive, and not all may apply to your situation. To gain a competitive edge on your competition, consider using the following approaches to possibly differentiate yourself:

- Volunteer for work projects and activities with your present employer
- Obtain additional credentials
- Speak a second language
- Stay up-to-date by reading trade publications
- Become a member of relevant organizations
- Attend conferences and seminars
- Become known in your field
- Earn a higher-level degree

VOLUNTEER AT WORK

Of all the above techniques, this is perhaps the easiest yet most often overlooked opportunity for differentiation. In every organization, management will periodically seek volunteers for various tasks. These activities may be totally work-oriented, such as being part of a special project or serving on a new committee, or may be related to a community or charitable cause with which the organization wants to be associated. Either way, volunteering for such endeavors will frequently provide you with:

- A chance to demonstrate or acquire skills outside those used in your routine day-to-day job.
- The opportunity to rub elbows with and get to know top organizational leaders with whom you would otherwise never meet or have access.
- Recognition of your name by leadership, reinforcing the notion you are a valuable employee who is willing to step forward when needed.

Management will sometimes mentally, and perhaps unintentionally, put good, high-performing people in a "box" and never think of them working in a capacity outside of their usual role. Consider the story of the following fictional employee.

Mary was an excellent warehouse inventory clerk, but management had no idea of her organizational and leadership skills until she volunteered to coordinate the charity fundraiser dinner for the company. To arrange this event, Mary communicated regularly by email and telephone with various leaders throughout the organization. These people worked in multiple areas of the company and were individuals with whom she would never normally have the need to interact. Top company leadership was present at the dinner, and the executive vice-president was the guest speaker.

Just think of all the top organizational leaders who now know Mary by name and are aware of the skills and energy she demonstrated. The next time Mary applies for a promotional opportunity outside of the warehouse, perhaps the interviewers may have heard of her or even worked with her on planning the dinner. Depending on the rapport she developed with many in top management during the charitable event, some of these individuals may be willing to serve as impressive professional references. There are never any guarantees, but Mary has likely differentiated herself favorably from the rest of the crowd of applicants. Management can now "see" Mary working in a role outside of her usual warehouse duties.

Volunteering is an effective, no-cost differentiation approach available to just about anyone. Plus, when management asks for volunteers, most employees usually duck and cover!

ADDITIONAL CREDENTIALS

Some career fields clearly prefer the "alphabet soup" of credentials. In other words, the more letters you have after your name, the better. If your field requires or at least favors one certification, license, or credential, are there others that would make sense to acquire as well? If the typical job applicant has one credential, would it help if you had more?

For example, in the insurance industry alone there are probably over two dozen professional designations one can earn. You may already have one or two, but depending on your situation, would it make sense for you to pursue others? Think about your resume compared to those of your competitors. Is it likely some of these individuals have more credentials? If credentials are a big deal in your field, you need to make yourself look better than the competition.

SPEAK A SECOND LANGUAGE

Sprechen sie Deutsch? ¿Habla español? Do you already speak one or more foreign languages? If so, use this to your advantage! With larger firms often being multinational in nature, the ability to speak additional languages can be a valuable and differentiating asset to an applicant. Several individuals I know communicate with foreign countries daily by telephone or email in the usual course of their jobs. As some positions may require occasional or even frequent visits to foreign countries, knowing the native language can make such trips much easier for the traveler and more effective in conducting business.

Even if the job does not require communicating in another language or traveling to other countries, being bilingual can be advantageous. For example, a company may have customers who are not proficient in English. These individuals may have a hard time ordering or understanding products or services, and having someone on staff who can communicate effectively with them is highly desirable.

Consider how this can be important in other fields as well, such as healthcare. Sometimes there are patients who speak little or no English. Most people are naturally apprehensive when it comes to being a patient, but imagine not being able to understand anything a physician, nurse, or other caregiver is trying to explain. Additionally, healthcare providers are obligated to ensure patients can make informed decisions about the care they receive, and the ability to effectively communicate obviously plays a critical role.

Given this possibility, it is not uncommon for hospitals and other healthcare providers to have an internal list of which staff can speak which languages. For example, a billing office clerk who can speak Arabic may be called upon to translate for a nurse attempting to explain something to a non-English speaking patient in the emergency room. Thus, for almost any job, having multilingual abilities in addition to the skills required for the position can make an applicant more appealing to an employer.

I am not suggesting you run right out and try to learn a second language (unless you want to) merely for differentiation purposes. Besides, in a work setting, an employer needs an individual fluent in a foreign language, not a beginner who can barely ask for directions to the train station. However, if you already speak another language, you may be able to put that skill to work for you as an applicant in many fields.

Similarly, do you know sign language? The ability to use sign language is another valuable skill you may possess that, for many of the reasons stated earlier, can be desirable to an employer and may help differentiate you from the other candidates.

Of course, if a job description *requires* the ability to speak or write a specific language, then it is not really a differentiating factor; it is just another minimum job requirement that all applicants must meet.

READ AND STAY UP-TO-DATE

One of the best ways to stay apprised of hot topics in a particular field is to read relevant trade publications. These will usually have articles regarding new applicable technologies, current trends, the potential impact of new or proposed regulations and laws, and other timely subjects. Subscriptions to some publications may be free while others can be quite expensive, so if possible, you may wish to access these through a public library. Also, an acquaintance working in your field may already receive such publications at work and just toss them after reading. Perhaps instead, they could give you the materials. Some periodicals (or at least excerpts) may also be available online, although a membership or subscription may be required for access.

If your interest is in the medical field, note that many hospitals, especially teaching hospitals, have excellent libraries housing various expensive periodicals and journals. Sometimes, even non-employees may be granted access to the medical library. While you may not be granted check-out privileges, you can at least read materials otherwise unavailable to the average job seeker. Your local public library may also be able to arrange loans of publications from other libraries where you may otherwise not be permitted physical access.

You might wonder how merely reading can help. For example, suppose the interviewer asks, "What do you think are the most important issues facing our industry today?" If you are up-to-date, you could likely mention one or two hot items. If the interviewer doesn't ask something like this, you could still bring up the subject when asked for questions. For example, suppose a new federal law is causing quite a stir in your field. You might ask, "I understand that new federal law #1234 is creating compliance problems for many companies in our field. Could you share how is this new law being addressed at this organization?" This enables you to demonstrate to the interviewers that you have above-average knowledge of current issues in the field. The fact that you are aware of current affairs and trends may help differentiate you from lesser-informed applicants.

ORGANIZATIONAL MEMBERSHIP

Membership in at least one relevant, recognized trade organization or association may help differentiate you and also provide benefits in several ways:

- Membership alone may help you stand out from the other applicants.
- Subscriptions to trade journals or online newsletters may be available only to members and included in the cost of membership.
- Members often receive discounts on publications and other materials.
- Members usually receive discounts to the organization's conferences, seminars, and online webinars.
- A local chapter may exist in your geographic area that can provide educational and networking opportunities.
- Members often have exclusive access to industry-specific job websites or job postings.

The cost of memberships can vary greatly. Some may be free, while others cost hundreds of dollars annually. When considering membership, check on the following:

- Some organizations offer membership to students at a significantly reduced price.
- It is not uncommon for some employers to pay for memberships.
- Memberships may be available on an individual or organizational basis; organizational memberships may permit a certain number of persons from the same company to join for a single price much lower than the cost of multiple individual memberships. Sometimes, only one membership fee is charged to an organization; after that, any other employee can join at no additional cost.

ATTEND CONFERENCES AND SEMINARS

Conferences and seminars may be conducted on a national or local basis, each with their own advantages. Regional and local meetings sometimes have lower registration costs than national events. Additionally, you may be able to commute to the site rather than incur the cost of airfare or a hotel. Especially due to the COVID-19 pandemic, virtual seminars have also become more commonplace.

National, in-person conferences, although often more expensive, offer many advantages. You will have the opportunity to meet and network with leaders from national organizations, colleagues, and prominent authors. Large national meetings typically host a wide variety of valuable educational sessions. Potential future employers may participate in a job fair and conduct interviews on-site (you may have to register separately for these). Frequently, these large meetings also host a sizable trade show where you can view the latest products and services. Such events can be both an educational resource bonanza and an enjoyable experience, but wear comfortable shoes—you will need them!

A large national meeting can also be just the thing to "recharge your batteries" and reinvigorate your passion for your field. Attending conferences and seminars helps demonstrate to current or potential employers that you are serious about your career. The resulting networking may not only help you learn of career opportunities elsewhere, but could give you a competitive advantage. Who knows? You might end up meeting individuals who could be your future job interviewers!

BECOME KNOWN IN YOUR FIELD

You might think this suggestion is like telling an unknown musician to suddenly become a rock star: easy to say, but nearly impossible to do. However, you may be surprised to learn there are actually several ways to do this. Consider the following:

- Large trade organizations are always looking for member volunteers to help organize and run national and local conferences, seminars, and meetings. Not only might you receive admission at lower or no cost, but you also gain additional networking opportunities during the process. You could also end up being named in the conference program as one of the organizers, resulting in national exposure.
- Most national conferences conduct a "Call for Papers/Presentations" well in advance of such large meetings. Is there a topic you could speak on? Perhaps describe an approach used at your current organization that would be of interest to others. I am not talking here about writing highly detailed research papers, and you do not have to be an "expert" in your field with numerous degrees and twenty years of experience. Just have something of interest to say or present a new and different spin on a topic. Often, copies or abstracts of all submitted papers are published in the conference "proceedings" document, even if the material was not selected for a full-blown live presentation. Your potential national exposure could be phenomenal, providing differentiation beyond what other applicants may have to offer. For example, I have personally submitted abstracts, papers, and presented several times at national conferences. On one such occasion, I won an award and a cash prize for the best presentation in my category. I also authored an article based on that presentation, which was subsequently published in a leading trade journal. As it turned out, the article then won another award and cash prize for the best published article for that year! This all happened simply because one day I decided to write and submit a paper.

- If you are extremely nervous about presenting to a large audience, consider a conference that also hosts "poster sessions." At these functions, participants prepare and display a poster containing information of interest to conference attendees. Poster sessions are typically walk-around type events, less formal or stressful. Specific times may be scheduled and set aside for conference attendees to meet and speak with the poster creators. Some poster sessions are judged, with awards presented. Since poster session participants are usually also named in the program or proceedings, you may gain recognition at a national level without ever having to speak to a large crowd. These sessions may also utilize large computer displays instead of physical posters to permit video content.
- National organizations that issue certification credentials frequently also offer a study guide for those interested in preparing and studying for the examination. If you already hold the certification, you may be able to volunteer to contribute to the study guide and thereby receive recognition in the process. The organization may have a "certification study guide committee" or some similar group of volunteers who draft review material, sample questions, or practice tests. As a contributor, you may be named as one of the authors or at least mentioned in the document.
- Consider teaching a class in your area of expertise. This might be anything from a formal university course to a community interest program open to anyone, and may be on a paid or volunteer basis. In addition to getting your name out there and becoming recognized, you will find that you personally learn a lot by teaching others.

EARN A HIGHER-LEVEL DEGREE

Properly written job descriptions will always indicate the educational requirements for a position. It is not uncommon for such requirements to include wording such as "Associate degree required; bachelor's degree preferred," or "Bachelor's degree required, master's degree preferred." In other words, they are specifying the minimum degree they will accept from an applicant but are also indicating the degree they would really like to see on the resume.

Having a higher-than-minimum level degree can help you in two ways. First, it can give you a competitive edge over other candidates who only meet the minimum educational requirements. Second, it might also enable the new employer to justify a higher starting salary for you than is usually offered.

Admittedly, most individuals do not necessarily have the time, money, or desire to pursue a higher-level degree. You may even still be working on completing your first degree. However, perhaps you were already considering obtaining additional education. Or, maybe you are in a work situation where realistically, you need to acquire a few more years of on-the-job experience before advancement would be possible. If so, pursuing advanced education in the interim could be a valuable career move that will benefit you for life. Plus, colleges today have so many nontraditional and flexible options (online programs, weekend-only programs, etc.) that pursuing additional education can sometimes literally be on your terms.

Having said the above, here are a few caveats regarding education. Avoid being so over-qualified academically that you look like an anomaly. For example, if a bachelor's degree is the norm in your field but it is not unusual to also have a master's degree, that would most likely be fine, probably even advantageous. However, having a PhD when an associate or bachelor's degree is clearly the norm may be problematic. Also, for entry-level positions, some employers may intentionally hire persons with the minimally-required degree to avoid paying a higher starting wage.

THE FINAL DIFFERENTIATION

Everything discussed here regarding differentiation may be helpful but is only part of the overall equation. The final and ultimate method of differentiation is the job interview. In the next chapters, interviewing will be discussed in depth.

YOUR PERSONAL READINESS: DIFFERENTIATION

- Have you taken opportunities in your current job to volunteer for projects, serve on committees, or engage in other activities that would highlight your skills and provide favorable exposure to management?
- Would additional applicable credentials, licenses, or certifications help differentiate you from other candidates?
- Do you speak any foreign languages?
- Do you stay up-to-date in your field by reading trade publications?
- Are you a member of relevant trade organizations and do you take advantage of their opportunities for education and networking?
- Do you attend conferences and seminars?
- Have you engaged in activities intended to give yourself state or national exposure, enabling you to become a recognized name in your field?
- Would pursuing additional education or a higher-level degree be possible and appropriate?

Interviewing (Part 1): Pre-Interview Considerations

Olympians train for years before they finally step into the arena to compete. Like them, you are now facing the ultimate test of your skill and preparation—the job interview. Although a gold medal may not await you, a job offer would be the perfect prize! However, just like an athlete, you do not want to drop the ball in this competition for which you have so diligently prepared.

As a readiness factor, interviewing covers a wide range of separate but critical topics. Using the one-bite-at-a-time approach to eating this elephant, the various topics comprising this factor will be presented in several parts over the next few chapters.

Part 1: Pre-Interview Considerations

First You Have to Get an Interview
What Constitutes a Good Fit?
Cover Your Bases
Resume or CV?
Professional References
Transcripts Can Be Tricky
If They Can't See It, They Can't Read It
Online Applications
Will Your Social Media Help or Hurt?

Part 2: The Interview Itself

Physical Interview Logistics
Go Prepared
Show and Tell
Interview Classification
Interview Types
Interview Formats
Answering Questions
It's Your Turn to Ask Questions
Eye Contact Mistakes
Should I Negotiate Salary During the Interview?
Ageism and the Older Applicant

Part 3: Post-Interview

Debrief
Thank the Interviewers
What if You Didn't Get the Job?

FIRST YOU HAVE TO GET AN INTERVIEW

Before you can put your interviewing skills to work, you first have to actually get an interview. Many applicants seem to skim over this basic but critical fact and conduct their job searches as if they can just crank out some resumes and letters and complete a few online applications. Then, like magic, they expect the interview invitations to start pouring in. So, before focusing on the interview itself, you must consider a few preliminary aspects.

I have been surprised over the years by the number of interview participants who appear to have, at best, only a minimal familiarity with the position for which they are applying. This seems rather odd, as job descriptions for posted positions are often available on the employer's website. If someone is planning to leave one job to take another, you would think they would at least read the job description in detail. But no, the evidence suggests otherwise. This may be why there are so many applicants who never even receive an invitation to interview. Perhaps they were so unfamiliar with the position that their application materials failed to demonstrate how they were a good match for the job.

Human resource departments and hiring managers have the daunting task of needing to quickly screen a huge number of applications—perhaps hundreds—and they are looking for individuals who clearly meet at least the minimum requirements and appear to be a good fit with the needs and duties of the position. As an applicant, if you expect to receive an interview invitation, you need to help the employer see right away when reviewing your application materials that you are a potential good fit.

WHAT CONSTITUTES A GOOD FIT?

Think about the task of shopping for a new computer, tablet, or smartphone. You probably already know the many needs the new device must fill, and now the challenge is to find a model that meets those needs. Depending on the type of device being purchased, the intended use (work or personal), and your own technical skill level, you might be examining each for features or specifications including:

- Screen size
- Physical size/weight
- Operating system
- Memory size
- Processor type/speed

- Battery life
- Software compatibility
- Ease of use
- Price
- Connectivity (USB, Bluetooth, HDMI, etc.)

When shopping, your approach likely involves looking at the available device choices and seeing how many of your requirements each product meets. Of course, you would like to find one which clearly meets *all* your needs, but sometimes that is just not possible. You might have to compromise by selecting one which meets *most* of your needs. The same holds true with employers. Many times, what an employer really wants in an applicant and what they are offered by the candidates from whom they actually receive applications may be two entirely different things. Unless the fit offered by all applicants is completely unacceptable, the search may become a compromise of determining which candidate meets at least most of their needs. Again, your goal is to demonstrate you are a good fit and that the employer should look at you closer by calling you in for an interview.

There is a school of thought promoting the notion that a resume is a "one-size-fits-all" document and the cover letter is where any customization should take place. This approach might work in situations where every job being sought is an identical, cookie-cutter position and the needs among different potential employers are essentially the same. However, in general, I disagree with this methodology and believe each potential employment opportunity deserves the effort of modifying any of your application materials as needed. Also, as you will discover later, a cookie-cutter resume will likely not fare well with the automated online application systems commonly in use.

If a human resources department is doing its part by posting well-written, accurate, and up-to-date job descriptions, identifying the position needs should be a relatively simple task. First, *thoroughly* read the job description and then *address each need* in your application materials. When reviewing a job description, examine how it relates to each of the following four readiness factors: Education, Experience, Skills, and Credentials.

Below is a short excerpt from an actual job posting. This position happens to be for a financial analyst supporting the facilities (buildings) for this organization. Regardless of your specific career field, use this example as an opportunity to practice examining and identifying the needs of this particular employer.

> **Individual tasks related to the duty.**
> - Participate in the development and implementation of facility budgets and expenditures including tracking and monitoring of facility budget and expenditures and making financial projections.
> - Prepare and track facility capital outlay work orders, maintenance work orders, miscellaneous operating projects, and agency inter-account billings. Track/reconcile budgets/expenditures on a statewide and per project basis.
> - Analyze, track, monitor, and report on all facilities related budgets, expenditures, and processes.
> - Utilize computer applications, software, databases, and report writing including, but not limited to, MS Excel, MS Access, MS PowerPoint, and Business Objects.
> - Provide and comply with extensive reporting requirements including, but not limited to, capital outlay, special

Based on the excerpt, what specifics would you mention in your resume and cover letter? You may wish to go through this posting and highlight the specific words and phrases that appear to represent their highest-priority needs.

Based on the information found in the posting, at a minimum, your application materials need to clearly indicate your experience with the following duties:

- Developing and implementing facilities budgets and expenditures.
- Analyzing, tracking, and monitoring facility budgets and expenditures.
- Making financial projections.
- Preparing and tracking facility capital outlay work orders, maintenance work orders, and miscellaneous operating projects.
- Utilizing computer applications, software, and databases such as MS Excel, MS Access, MS PowerPoint, and Business Objects.

Although only a few specific items are shown in the example, you get the idea and probably noticed the words selected were taken directly from the job description. It is important to "speak their language" because during the application review process the employer is looking for these specific terms. A later section regarding automated online application systems will describe and reinforce why this need for wording consistency is so important.

If the job description states "participated," be careful not to say "helped" or some other word that may de-emphasize your role in the eyes of the reviewer. When the job description includes the need to "analyze, track, and monitor" certain financial parameters, it implies the individual will be personally responsible for performing these tasks. Given this, you would not want to indicate that you "assisted." Instead, clearly state you were responsible for performing these duties.

Some application reviewers analyze and critique the wording of applicants to the extreme. For example, if the job description states you must be "proficient" in the use of certain software, do not merely state that you have "used" it or are "familiar with" the software. Simply having used a particular application or being familiar with it is not the same as being able to utilize it proficiently. Some resume reviewers will approach it exactly that way and nitpick your wording.

Along these same lines, be careful with acronyms or buzz words. While these might be familiar in your current job, they may have no meaning to the reviewer of your application. Consider the following statement:

"I have compiled reports including FMBR and WOBR, and documentation as required by Section 102.33, using applications in Microsoft Office and report writer software."

From your perspective, the above statement regarding your current job duties and experience may be absolutely true and accurate. This terminology might be acceptable when applying for a position within your own department with your present employer, or if the terms are commonly used in your field. However, to someone outside of your organization or field, these words may sound like meaningless gibberish. A reviewer might read the above statement and wonder:

- What were the types of reports?
- Did the applicant actually create these reports or merely compile the work of others?
- What are FMBR, WOBR, and Section 102.33?
- Which specific Microsoft Office applications did the applicant use?
- Which specific report writer applications did the applicant use?

After pondering these questions for all of maybe two seconds, odds are the reviewer placed this application in the "unqualified" pile. Why? Because the applicant failed to show how they are a good fit for the needs and requirements of the position. Besides, there are probably other applicants who clearly demonstrated their fit more convincingly. Unless the job posting mentions the exact acronyms or terms and you are absolutely sure they will be understood, do not use them. Statements in your application materials that include wording consistent with those found in the posted job description will be much more convincing to a potential interviewer.

COVER YOUR BASES

Once you identify the needs and requirements of a position, make sure your application materials clearly demonstrate your fit.

- Education: Make it clear how you meet the specific education and training requirements.
- Experience: Describe how your work experience is relevant. If a specific amount of on-the-job time is required, indicate how you meet or exceed it.
- Skills: If the job description calls for specific skill sets or abilities, make it clear you have them.
- Credentials: If specific credentials such as licenses, certifications, etc., are required or preferred, identify which you possess.

It may seem job applications, especially those online, are more complex and time-consuming than doing your income taxes! Yet, despite all the effort needed to complete these lengthy applications, many job seekers simply end up wasting their time. This is because applicants often do not include all the required files or attachments. These might consist of a cover letter, resume, college transcripts, professional references, letters of recommendation, or whatever else the employer may specifically require at the time of submission. *If the employer requires something up front, include it at the time of submission!* Failing to do so often means immediate and automatic exclusion from further consideration.

RESUME OR CV?

Not surprisingly, job applicants are typically required to submit a resume. In some cases, the posting allows submission of either a resume or a document known as a "CV." Other times, the posting may specifically require a CV. So, what exactly is a CV, and how does it differ from a resume? When might a CV be preferred over a resume?

The abbreviation CV is short for the Latin phrase "Curriculum Vitae," which translates to "course of life." When speaking, most people just use the abbreviation "CV." However, if you wish to use the Latin words, the two most commonly accepted pronunciations are:

curriculum "vee-tie" or curriculum "vye-tee"

As you already know, a typical resume might include information such as:

- Education: where and when you went to high school and/or college, degrees received, GPA and/or noteworthy academic awards.
- Employment history: current and past organizations for whom you have worked, the dates of employment, the positions you held and associated duties, and noteworthy job accomplishments.
- Credentials: applicable licenses, certifications, etc.
- Applicable professional or other work-related organizations of which you are a member.

Unless an applicant is very experienced and has significant work history and education, a resume is traditionally kept to one page in length (one side of one page). Even experienced applicants usually keep their resumes to no more than two pages (both sides of one page). Why? The people who review incoming resumes (managers, HR representatives, recruiters, etc.) usually have to process numerous submissions. They simply do not have the time or desire to read a lengthy document for each applicant.

Although opinions are mixed about whether or not this should be done, resumes are often revised or tailored as needed to best fit a particular position for which one may be applying. In my opinion, a resume should not be "carved in stone." I see no problem in making a few adjustments to one's resume to enhance or highlight certain aspects that may be of interest to a specific employer. However, a resume that is well-written in the first place should only need minor tweaks. Certainly, it should not require a complete overhaul every time it is used.

Like a resume, the CV contains the same employment, education, and other information described earlier, but in more detail. However, this is where the similarity ends. Unlike a resume, the scope of the CV is much broader and includes additional information such as:

- A bibliography (a list of papers, abstracts, articles, books, or other publications the applicant has authored).
- Specialized education or advanced training, including internships, residencies, fellowships, etc.
- Specialized skills, such as languages spoken or advanced computer software or programming abilities.
- Titles, dates, and locations (including city, state, conference or organization name, etc.) of presentations or speeches given by the applicant.
- Various work-related, academic, community, or professional association committees or boards on which the applicant has served and the role (e.g., chairperson, treasurer, etc.).
- College classes, courses, seminars, or other training programs developed and/or taught by the applicant.
- Various grants, awards, or other recognitions the applicant has received.
- Professional references (resumes usually do not contain professional references).

Because a CV is intentionally more detailed, it may often fill numerous pages. A typical CV likely has a length of about three to five pages. However, some very experienced professionals may have CVs of 15 or more pages. So, why is it acceptable for this document to be so much longer than a resume? Simple: because the employer specifically asking for a CV wants and expects to see that level of detail.

A CV may be thought of as an extensive biographical profile of an individual's life and career. Thus, unlike a resume, it is not modified to fit each new job application. Of course, the CV is updated as needed whenever the individual has new and relevant content to add.

Typically, CVs are almost exclusively used in academia, medicine, science, and research. These fields place very high importance on an applicant having significant amounts of education, teaching experience, authoring of papers, service on committees, and so forth. Because the CV is the format of choice for presenting such information, it is usually the document requested by employers for positions in such fields.

However, even within these fields in general, the document expected by the employer depends on the position sought. Unless the posting states otherwise, most positions normally thought of as "regular jobs" call for a resume, not a CV. For example, an individual applying for a billing position in a medical clinic or hospital would typically send a resume, not a CV, even though the job may be related to the medical field. Similarly, a person applying for an administrative assistant job in a university physics department would also likely send a resume rather than a CV, as the position does not directly involve teaching or scientific research.

Which document type should you submit with your application? Simple; whichever is requested in the job posting. However, there is an important caveat. The differences between resumes and CVs as described above tend to apply to the United States (US) and Canada, but not necessarily everywhere else. In some countries, the terms "CV" and "resume" may be used interchangeably. Still, in other countries, submitting a full-blown CV may be the norm when applying for a job that would only call for a basic resume in the US or Canada. Do some research online and determine what information the employer in that country is looking for and expects. You certainly would not want to send a potential employer an eight-page CV when what they expected was the American equivalent of a simple, one-page resume.

Here in the United States, we take for granted that most personal information should not be included on resumes and CVs. Most applicants know it is illegal for an employer to ask for such details, and many of us would be shocked and appalled if an employer were to ask during a job interview, "So, are you married?" or "Exactly how old are you?" But such information is not necessarily off-limits in other parts of the world. When applying for positions in other countries, be sure to research their expectations for the type of personal information to be included. Then, decide whether you are willing to provide such details as a precondition of being considered for the job.

Unless your career involves the fields of academia, medicine, science, or research, or you are applying for certain international positions, chances are you will not be asked to submit a CV. So, was learning about CVs a waste of your time? Not at all. Here's why: First, you now know the differences between the two documents and when each may be the right tool to use. Second, you are now better prepared to consider developing a CV as a personal resource. Let me explain.

Developing a CV for your personal use can be a helpful exercise in documenting all the various accomplishments of your career. As you gain experience over the years, easily forgotten details such as exact dates, locations, names, etc. will start to fade. While you may never submit the CV itself for a position, it can still serve as a useful reference when you are fine-tuning a resume or preparing for a job interview. Instead of having to look up the detailed information each time you need it—assuming you can even find it again—you will have it ready at your fingertips. Plus, should you decide someday to teach at a college or university, even part-time, they will likely want you to provide a CV, not a resume.

PROFESSIONAL REFERENCES

If you have a list of professional references or need to mention individuals as references on your application, be sure:

- Anyone on your list has given their approval, in advance, to be included. *This is critical!*
- The contact information for each person is accurate and up-to-date.
- The individuals can be trusted to speak positively about you.

These may seem like common-sense details, but they are often ignored by applicants. What would an interviewer think if the contacted reference was surprised by the call and had absolutely no idea they were on your list? When this happens, the reference may not be willing to speak at all, and if they are, they may sound suspiciously cautious. In today's litigious, sue-me-sue-you environment, people are understandably hesitant to say almost anything to an unexpected and unknown caller seeking employment information, especially if asked probing questions about your personality, abilities, skills, etc.

Also, what does it say about your attention to detail when every reference the interviewer attempts to contact has an invalid email address, a non-working telephone number, or has since left the company or retired? The easier you make it for the interviewer to obtain the necessary reference checks, the better. Additionally, it may be possible more than one candidate is being considered for the job you seek. Don't let your competition win out simply because no one could reach your references, making you look like the less desirable applicant.

The last point regarding trusting the reference to speak positively about you may seem rather obvious, but apparently not to everyone. I once called a candidate's listed reference who proceeded to describe how the individual had been involved in several physical altercations and fistfights on the job.

Maintain your list of professional references as a separate document, keep it updated, and provide it only upon request. Others may disagree, but I recommend indicating "Professional references available upon request" at the end of your resume. However, do not place the references themselves on the resume. Also, do not routinely send the list of references along with cover letters, resumes, and applications unless the job posting or online application system instructs you to do so. Be sure to take several copies of your professional reference list along with you to the job interview. If interviewers are sufficiently impressed with you to want to check references right away, having your list immediately available both speeds up the process and makes you look even better.

Go for quality of references, not quantity. In cases where it would be applicable and appropriate to do so, consider using professionals from different disciplines. For example, someone applying for a position in a hospital setting may wish to have a mix that includes their supervisor, a physician, a nurse, and a hospital administrator, rather than four individuals who all hold the exact same position.

Do not write a detailed or lengthy narrative for each name listed. Include extra information only if it is needed to clarify something. I usually suggest including prefixes such as "Mr.," "Ms.," or other clues to indicate the gender of the individual being contacted, especially for names that may be common to both sexes or those which are unusual or foreign. Doing so can help avoid potential embarrassment for both the interviewer and the called party.

Having said that, however, be aware that due to sensitivity regarding sexual orientation and gender identity, there is a growing movement toward eliminating the use of gender-specific terms altogether. For example, it is becoming more common for biographies on company websites to include a list of an individual's preferred pronouns (e.g., he, his, him). Attitudes about indicating gender seem to vary considerably, so research the acceptability of using gender-specific wording in your situation before drafting your list of references. The last thing you want to do when applying for a position is to accidentally offend either your reference or the interviewer, even though that was certainly not your intent.

A stand-alone list of professional references might be formatted as shown on the next page. Notice how additional comments were included where helpful and applicable. Again, you will want to modify or eliminate the pronouns or other gender-specific terms if you sense this is an issue for the individuals involved.

Professional References

John D. Doe
1234 Main St.
Mytown, NY 12345
Cell: (233) 555-0100

Mr. John D. Bigshot, President and CEO
Big City Central Manufacturing Inc.
5432 Old Oak Park Drive
Big City, NJ 07102
John.Bigshot@bcctymfg.com
Office: (890) 555-0133

Ms. Chris Thompson, Chief Operating Officer
Amalgamated Products Ltd.
2020 Industrial Ave.
Detroit, MI 48211
MThompson2001X@amprltd.com
Office: (329) 555-0199
Cell: (329) 555-0124
Note: Ms. Thompson was my supervisor in her previous position as
Production Manager with Big City Central Manufacturing Inc.

Mr. Leslie Rodgerson (Retired)
2222 Jump St.
Tampa, FL 33601
GoneFishing23589@sscable.net
Home: (624) 555-0108
Cell: (624) 555-0114
Note: Mr. Rodgerson was my supervisor in his former position
as Sales Manager with Big IT Products.

Professor Pat Appleseed, PhD
Professor of Business Administration
Getcher Degree College
6245 Tuition Way
Some City, CA 90001
P.Appleseed322@getcher.edu
Office: (558) 555-0172
Note: Professor Appleseed was my faculty advisor for a
semester-long project in her Marketing 501 course.

IF THEY CAN'T SEE IT, THEY CAN'T READ IT

If you want your required attachments to be viewable, make sure they are in a software format the employer accepts. The job posting will typically indicate the preferred or required file formats, such as Microsoft Word or PDF. Automated online application systems need your materials to be submitted in a particular file format in order to accurately scan and electronically process them. Since online application systems are the norm, a later section will examine some of the behind-the-scenes ramifications this technology may have for unsuspecting applicants.

If you are using software that outputs files in a format different from what is requested, convert the files to the necessary format and be sure to check the results, proofreading everything before sending. Conversion from one file type to another will sometimes unexpectedly change fonts or alter formatting, such as spacing, margins, line breaks, symbol characters, and so forth, with the end result not being anything close to what you expected or wanted.

I know a job seeker who applied for numerous positions and sent out nearly 100 cover letters and resumes to various companies by email. Unfortunately, this occurred right after the release of a major software update. At first, a backward compatibility problem existed. For a while, files created by the latest version of the software could not be read by older versions, and most employers had not yet upgraded. Further, the applicant had recently purchased a brand-new laptop, and—you guessed it—the preloaded word processor software was the latest version, which automatically saved everything in the new file format.

As a result of this "perfect storm" of events, only a few of the 100 recipients could open or automatically process the attachments. The applicant discovered this sad fact only after a few companies were kind enough to reply, indicating they could not open the attachments. Of course, most companies simply deleted the unreadable files.

Also, I cannot emphasize enough the importance of proofing and checking whatever materials you send. Many applicants will have friends, mentors, and others review and critique their cover letters, resumes, and other materials, attempting to polish the documents and put their best foot forward. Since this process is frequently handled via email for convenience, the individuals performing the review may use the "track changes" features of the word processing software. This handy function enables reviewers to comment and suggest changes and improvements. However, once all changes are complete, producing a final document cleared of all comments and suggestions can sometimes be challenging, especially for inexperienced users.

I recall a job applicant who electronically submitted a cover letter and resume, unaware that the change tracking feature's annotations had not been correctly cleared. As a result, the interviewer received the materials complete with every single edit, comment, and suggestion clearly shown on the documents. How embarrassing!

TRANSCRIPTS CAN BE TRICKY

Applicants may sometimes find themselves in a predicament regarding college or high school transcripts. Employers may state "official" transcripts are required, which are usually sent directly to them by the college or university. Applicants typically have little or no control over how quickly this will actually happen. Frequently, every separate transcript request to a college must be made in writing, and it is not uncommon for there to be a fee for each one sent. So how does one comply?

I have seen postings that avoid the problem altogether by requiring that transcripts must be submitted at the time of application, but these may initially be unofficial copies. Official transcripts from the college must be submitted later, if and when an applicant is under serious consideration. When an official transcript is required up front and you cannot comply for some reason, contact the Human Resources department (or other stated contact) of the potential employer. See if they would be willing to accept an unofficial version until the official copy can be provided by the college.

ONLINE APPLICATIONS

Applicants search job postings, polish their resumes and cover letters, and begin applying for open positions in hopes of securing an interview. Spoiler alert! Who said submitting even well-written application materials would result in these documents ever actually being read? Many applicants feel that applying online is like sending their applications into a black hole, never to be seen again.

The modern job application process can feel like a virtual obstacle course. It is designed, at least in part, to screen out unqualified individuals up front, thereby reducing the number of applications the employer will need to review and process. Human resources (HR) departments and employers are always looking for ways to identify those applicants who are simply not a good match for the posted job or do not meet the minimum requirements. Finding efficient methods to screen applicants has become more urgent for several reasons:

- The number of applications employers receive for any single position since the arrival of the internet and online job postings has multiplied tremendously. It is not uncommon for any one listing, even for a lower-level job, to receive hundreds of applications or more.
- More and more people seem to apply for jobs—any posted jobs—even when they clearly do not meet the minimum requirements. This may be out of desperation, dissatisfaction with their current jobs, or perhaps because actively applying for positions may be required to continue receiving unemployment or other benefits.
- Like most other work areas, human resources departments have been subjected to budget cuts and downsizing over the years. As a result, they are likely to be understaffed relative to the volume of work they need to perform.

In larger organizations years ago, and even in some smaller ones today, applicant screening was assigned to a personnel analyst or technician in the HR department. This individual was tasked with reading each and every application and then comparing the information found in the cover letter and resume to the stated minimum requirements in the job description. For example, suppose the job description called for a minimum of three years of work experience. The analyst would examine the work history as stated on the resumes and applications to see if, in fact, each applicant actually possessed the required experience.

Over time, this intensely manual process became overwhelming as the number of applicants increased dramatically. Additionally, this task has been made even more difficult because applicants are often vague regarding the details of their work experience, and the wording of their stated college degree sometimes makes it unclear whether it is a match with the required degree.

Human resources software to the rescue! Well, at least in theory. Such software may consist of a stand-alone Applicant Tracking System (ATS) or as a module of a large, organization-wide Human Resources Management System (HRMS) or Human Resources Information System (HRIS). As you might imagine, numerous such products are offered by both large and small software companies.

The idea behind these systems goes like this: Online applicants submit their resumes, cover letters, etc., and answer questions about their education, experience, and other job requirements. The software can then scan these materials, looking for the presence and/or frequency of particular keywords and phrases, and review the responses to questions. The resulting data for applicants can then be automatically entered into a database, with an overall score for each. The attached cover letter and resume files are electronically filed away for later review if needed. Once the position posting has closed, the database can be queried by the HR person to display the names and information of only those candidates who scored well and met specific criteria.

Although each ATS works somewhat differently, the end goal is the same: to automate the initial review of job applications to the greatest extent possible. For example, suppose a posted job requires three years of experience as a "customer service representative." An ATS screening question regarding work experience might read:

Do you have a minimum of three years of experience as a customer service representative?

☐ Yes
☐ No

Or,

How many years of experience do you have as a customer service representative?

☐ 0 - 1
☐ 2 - 3
☐ 4 - 5
☐ More than 5

Assume 150 applications have been received, and to keep things manageable, the hiring department only wants to interview between five and ten candidates. Also, assume the question is worded as shown in the second example above, with multiple-choice responses. Logically, HR may wish to first identify the candidates with the most experience, as these individuals might be considered the best qualified. Therefore, the database will be queried by HR to output only the names of those applicants who answered with "More than 5" years of customer service experience.

What if, when filtered in this manner, the database yields only three names? Clearly, this does not meet the desired number of candidates requested by the hiring department. To increase the number of possible interviewees, the database is queried again, but this time search is expanded to also include applicants with "4 to 5" years of customer service experience. Suppose the system now identifies five additional applicants, resulting in a total of eight potential interviewees. HR is satisfied, as this is consistent with the number of applicants the client area wishes to interview.

In reality, the screening process likely does not end there. Any number of other criteria might be used in combination to further qualify and filter the applicants. For example, suppose the job posting requires a minimum of an associate degree with a preference for those with a bachelor's degree. In this case, the employer may wish to also filter the education parameter and identify only candidates who possess bachelor's degrees.

Aside from completing the online application, a job posting may have several additional requirements. These may include submitting a resume, cover letter, a college transcript, and providing written answers to specific supplemental questions. Failure to include any one of these required items will result in immediate exclusion from further consideration, which is another type of filtering. Shown below is an excerpt from an actual online job posting for a high school teaching position.

> To Apply: Submit a letter of interest, resume, letters of recommendation, transcripts and valid teaching certificate electronically or by mail to:

In addition to the scanning needs of the ATS, any number of various document types may also be required up front for several reasons:

- Applicants who do not include the required attachments may be assumed to lack attention to detail and demonstrate they cannot follow directions. Obviously, neither characteristic is desirable in a candidate.
- Cover letters and written responses to supplemental questions provide interviewers with an opportunity to evaluate applicants' writing and communication skills, if such skills are important and relevant to the position.
- The HR department does not have the time to follow up later with applicants to obtain such documents, so these items are required when the application is submitted.

Returning to the example above, assume filtering the database for a bachelor's degree eliminated two more applicants, and one of the remaining candidates failed to include a cover letter. This reduces the initial pool of eight applicants down to five. This number still meets the desired minimum number of candidates to be interviewed. Therefore, HR sends these five applications to the hiring area manager for review and possible selection for an interview.

Thanks to the ATS, the otherwise enormously time-consuming task of individually screening all 150 initial applications has essentially become automated. The number of HR staff needed to process the applications is reduced, and the system speeds up the turnaround time for processing the applications. Unfortunately, human eyes will only see the applications of just those five final candidates. No matter how compelling the cover letters, resumes, and additional materials of the other applicants may have been, the files of those remaining 145 applicants will likely never even be opened or reviewed by a real person.

Another potential benefit of automated screening, especially in today's litigious environment, is that it may offer at least some protection and defense against charges of discrimination in hiring practices. I am not an attorney, but it seems reasonable that if candidates are selected for interviews without regard to race, based strictly upon specific, objective, valid, work-related criteria, then such a process might help defend the organization in the event of a lawsuit.

Similarly, this process also makes it harder for a racist or biased manager to discriminate against applicants based on information they might glean by reading the documents of every single applicant. With the ATS, many applications may be received, but most are rejected or scored low by the system, with only a few chosen. However, all applicants are evaluated fairly and consistently and ranked objectively by the ATS software. Because only the files of those few who meet specific criteria are ever actually opened and read, there is less chance of human bias.

However, it is important to note using an ATS does not necessarily guarantee that a hiring process is free of discrimination. For example, should the organizational hiring process itself, whether automated or not, be found to somehow systematically exclude individuals of legally protected classes, even if such exclusion is unintentional, the courts may still find the employer guilty of discrimination. This is a very dynamic area in which laws and court decisions are ever-evolving.

For many reasons, it is evident the automated online application process is here to stay, as it is efficient, reduces costs, and results in overall faster service from the HR department. Such systems and software should ensure the best candidates are identified and make life easier for both HR departments and hiring managers, right? Perhaps in a perfect world, this might be true; however, there are a few issues:

- Many professionals feel that, overall, the ATS software developed to date does a less-than-optimal job of identifying the best candidates, frequently screening out perfectly acceptable individuals for various technical reasons.
- People are often dishonest when answering employment application questions.
- Not all applicants interpret online application questions or requirements in the same way, resulting in inconsistent responses.
- The questions asked in the online application may be worded in a vague or unclear manner, again resulting in invalid ranking variations.

Since ATS applications utilize automated searches for specific words and phrases, some are not robust enough to accommodate the wording variations used by applicants. If the software is scanning a resume for the specific phrase "five years of experience in database administration and development of data tables," and the applicant writes, "worked 10 years managing and creating databases," the resume might receive a low score by the system even though the candidate is completely qualified. Some systems may have quirks, such as being sensitive to the order in which certain information is placed on a resume or the headings used.

Also, not all systems may be able to scan all document types. For example, if the software is optimized for use with Microsoft Word files and the applicant submits PDFs instead, the ATS may score this individual as a poor fit because it cannot effectively recognize the file content. *This is an important reason to always submit your files in the format requested by the employer!* Despite advances in this technology, qualified applicants can—and do—fall between the cracks, and organizations sometimes miss out on potentially excellent candidates. To help reduce this possibility—but frustrating to applicants—some systems also require that the resume or other information be manually entered into an online form, in addition to submitting the materials electronically.

Unfortunately, not all candidates answer each application question truthfully. Some people have learned how to "game" HR software to ensure they make it through the first round of filtering. It is really quite easy; just answer every question with a response the employer will consider most favorable! Consider the following hypothetical online ATS questions an accounting applicant might be required to answer:

1. How many years of experience do you have working as an accountant?

    ☐ 0 - 1
    ☐ 2 - 3
    ☐ 4 - 5
    ☐ More than 5

2. How many years of experience do you have using Microsoft Excel?

    ☐ 0 - 1
    ☐ 2 - 3
    ☐ 4 - 5
    ☐ More than 5

3. How would you rate your skill level using Microsoft Excel?

    ☐ Beginner
    ☐ Intermediate
    ☐ Advanced
    ☐ Expert

4. How would you rate your understanding of current FASB standards?

    ☐ Beginner
    ☐ Intermediate
    ☐ Advanced
    ☐ Expert

Faced with the questions above, a dishonest candidate would automatically answer "More than 5" for questions one and two, regardless of their actual amount of experience. Similarly, they would answer questions three and four as "Expert" regardless of their actual level of skill or understanding. In fact, the applicant may not even be familiar with the FASB acronym (Financial Accounting Standards Board). Acronyms may sometimes be used deliberately in job postings to discourage unqualified individuals who do not understand them.

By intentionally answering the questions dishonestly, the applicant is more likely to show up in the first list of well-qualified candidates produced by the system. If nothing further is done to evaluate the honesty of the answers through a manual review of the application materials, the individual might even be offered an interview. Depending on the organization, and especially if HR has total control over the recruitment process, the answers may be accepted at face value (for now) even if the resume does not appear to support them. In such a situation, HR may push the task of documenting the candidate as unqualified onto the interviewer, resulting in unnecessary, time-wasting interviews.

Fortunately, most applicants are honest and do not deliberately falsify their materials. However, a candidate may simply have an unrealistic or dissimilar idea of what constitutes acceptable experience or a proficient skill level. For example, an applicant who has worked eight years in a very small company as a part-time bookkeeper may feel this constitutes "corporate accounting" experience; however, the employer may think such experience must include high-level accounting skills and financial report preparation for regulatory audits.

Similarly, candidates may have unrealistic perceptions of their own skill levels. A candidate barely able to create a simple chart in a spreadsheet may genuinely believe they possess "advanced" Excel skills. However, the employer may be looking for someone who can write macros in VBA code and develop complex formulas using nested functions. Although not a deliberate misrepresentation, this difference in interpretation produces a real "good fit" gap between the applicant and employer.

When any of the above situations exist, the first round of interviews will not go well for either the candidates or the employer. Many hours will be wasted interviewing candidates unable to articulate or demonstrate the level of skill or experience claimed in their online applications. When this happens, a second filtering of the remaining applicants will likely need to occur, requiring a second round of interviews.

At this point, you may be thinking:

- If I game the electronic application process, I have a higher chance of securing an interview.
- If I answer honestly, I may just get lost in the crowd of applicants.

While both of the above statements may be true to some extent, my advice is to ALWAYS answer the questions honestly, regardless of the potential outcome. Your integrity is at stake here. The interview is the only chance you will have to make a good impression. I can tell you from experience that interviewers are absolutely disgusted with applicants who have obviously lied on their applications. Yes, these individuals may have tricked their way into a job interview, but be assured they will not be able to "wow" or fool the interviewers. In the end, such candidates merely demonstrate a lack of credibility, honesty, and integrity. They destroy any chance of being hired—now or later. So, in the end, what was gained by trying to game the system?

When completing an online application, answer the questions in a way you would be able to substantiate during an interview. If a question offers an opportunity to write an answer and explain (such as, "Describe your experience in this line of work"), be specific and clear. Make it evident to the reader that you know what you are talking about. An experienced interviewer need not ask tricky questions to learn the depth of an interviewee's knowledge. Usually, asking a question which just "scratches below the surface" will quickly reveal whether a candidate's level of knowledge has depth or if it is only superficial. An applicant who merely uses buzzwords or acronyms without a functional understanding of them will quickly be exposed. Consider the following dialogue for an electronics technician position, based on real interview experiences:

Candidate: *"In my current position, I have considerable experience using a digital multimeter to take voltage and current readings. While performing my work over the past three years, I have used one every day."*

Interviewer: *"That's great! What brand and model of digital multimeter did you use? Did it have an ammeter clamp?"*

Candidate: *"Um . . . er . . . I'm not sure . . . The meter is yellow."*

Think about it. The candidate boasts about having "considerable experience" with a particular piece of test equipment, supposedly used daily for the past three years, and then does not know anything about it other than it is yellow? Really? Aside from being disappointed, the interviewer may now feel other answers provided by the applicant are suspect as well. Also, the candidate likely is (or ought to be) embarrassed about being unable to answer such a basic question, especially after making such big claims of proficiency.

As a job-seeker who submits online applications, what can you do to maximize your chances of being offered an interview?

- Try to ensure sure your understanding of the job and its requirements is consistent with that of the employer by reading the job posting very carefully several times before answering the online questions. Then, answer the questions at the highest level you can honestly substantiate.
- When writing your resume and answering any online questions, use the same wording and phrases found in the job posting. If the posting states "professional experience," do not refer to it as "corporate experience" or "work experience." If it calls for experience with "Excel," do not just say "spreadsheet." Otherwise, the system may score your resume as a poor fit due to the mismatch of the wording used.
- Avoid using unusual fonts, graphics, or formats that may cause difficulty for ATS software and prevent it from properly extracting your data.
- Be sure to attach any required documents and ensure they are in the requested file format. Without them, your application may be immediately and automatically excluded from any further consideration. Before clicking the "Submit" button, double-check that all required items are attached. Depending on the position, these required attachments may include:

    - Cover letter
    - Resume
    - Curriculum vitae (CV)
    - One or more letter(s) of recommendation
    - Professional references
    - College transcript (check whether this must be official, or if unofficial is acceptable)
    - Answers to supplemental or essay-type questions
    - Copies of military training or discharge documents
    - Copies of credentials such as licenses, certifications, etc.

Due to automated systems, candidates today may have less influence on the application process than they would prefer. However, by following directions and carefully crafting their responses, applicants may be able to stay in the game.

Assuming an applicant has successfully navigated the online application obstacle course and received an invitation for an online or in-person job interview, what next? Pre-interview readiness may have helped impress the employer sufficiently to land the invitation, but now one must be ready to succeed in the interview itself. However, first, there is one more thing to consider.

WILL YOUR SOCIAL MEDIA HELP OR HURT?

Examining your social media with a critical eye is something you must do well in advance of an interview, in fact, even before your job search begins. What role does social media play in an interview?

When every candidate interviews equally well, an employer faces a tough decision. Often, before deciding who to hire, an interviewer will want to find out more about each finalist to determine what they are really like. They know you were on your best behavior during the interview, but the "real you" will come out once you are hired. How can they find out? Fortunately for them, this is a pretty easy task.

All an employer has to do to learn a lot about you is look on the internet, especially at social media sites. Perhaps they will learn more than you want them to know, and it does not even matter how much of it is true. Employers will likely assume that your online posts reveal the kind of person you really are, your unmasked attitudes about people and things. And they may not like what they see.

For example, did you drop the "F-bomb" in a few posts? Or post a picture of you partying a little too hard last weekend? That joke you posted might be considered by some as offensive, or some comment you made might smack of racism. Is this the real you they will see on the job?

Wait a minute. Check you out online? Can they do that? Isn't that illegal or something? I am not an attorney, so I cannot advise on legal matters. However, the U.S. Equal Employment Opportunity Commission (EEOC) website (www.eeoc.gov) has a wealth of information on such topics, including prohibited employment and hiring practices. It appears that, as long as an employer does not use anything they learn online in a manner that violates employment or discrimination laws, they can look all they want at your social media. Once you post something, it is public information. So, yes, employers CAN and DO look at the social media of their job applicants. All the time. In fact, a national online survey conducted by Harris Poll in 2017 on behalf of the website CareerBuilder.com[2] found:

- 70% of employers use social media to screen candidates before hiring
- 69% use online search engines such as Google, Yahoo, and Bing to research candidates

So, if that is the case, should your social media posts be strictly limited to cute puppy videos or pictures of you passing out food at the local homeless shelter? No, but think of it this way: *your online presence is essentially the other half of your resume.* Given that, use common sense and make sure your social media casts you in a positive and professional light. If it does not, take some time to try and clean up what is out there.

As most employers will research you after the interview, waiting until then to worry about your social media is obviously too late. You should take proactive steps before your job search even begins to optimize your online appearance. Here are some suggestions regarding social media:

- Think about the tone of your posts. Avoid drama, putting people down, vicious political attacks, or being a big whiner.
- Do not use language you would never use during a job interview.
- Do not post anything that makes you look irresponsible or suggests you overindulge in things.
- Never bad-mouth your current or previous job, employer, or customers.

On the flip side, you also do not want to be "off the grid" or invisible. If you cannot be found at all, or your privacy settings are so tight even the CIA cannot see anything, an employer might suspect you have something to hide. You want to have an online presence, but one that suggests you are a person an employer would be comfortable hiring.

YOUR PERSONAL READINESS: INTERVIEWING

➢ Do your cover letter and resume adequately reinforce how you are a good fit for the position?
➢ Does the position require a resume, or is a CV preferred?
➢ Is your list of professional references up to date?
➢ Do you have an unofficial copy of your college transcript available?
➢ Do you know the process involved in sending an official copy of your college transcript, if requested?
➢ Are your cover letter, resume, and other application materials ATS-friendly?
   o Do they use wording consistent with the job posting?
   o Do they avoid unusual formatting and graphics?
   o Have they been saved and submitted in the file format specified by the employer?
➢ Will your social media help or hurt your job search?

■ Interviewing (Part 2): The Interview Itself

Once invited to an interview, an applicant must be ready to jump the next job search hurdle: the interview itself. First, however, the candidate must get to the interview, regardless of whether it is physical or virtual. Each method has its own set of logistical issues to consider and address.

PHYSICAL INTERVIEW LOGISTICS

Do you know any punctually-challenged individuals? These are the people who, no matter what, for whatever reason, can never seem to be on time for anything, whether work-related or personal. It only stands to reason that some percentage of these same individuals will also show up late for job interviews. One might suspect these folks would modify their behavior for such an important event, but unfortunately, many do not. Arriving late to an interview might be unimaginable to you, and therefore you plan the logistics of your travel accordingly. Here are a few aspects of interview logistics that may be helpful.

Arriving late to an interview could be due to several reasons: a habit of poor punctuality, travel time miscalculation, unfamiliarity with the location, or events completely outside of your control. As for habit, that one is on you, but you can take steps to mitigate the impact of the other variables. The distance you must travel for the interview obviously affects which of the following issues are applicable and most important.

If the interview requires you to travel to a distant city, make sure your planned arrival time allows room for the unexpected. Any transportation mode can experience delays, and you always need to build a buffer into your travel time estimates. Unless you are already intimately familiar with the particular city, its traffic, and the transportation modes involved, always allow considerably more time than you think is needed. Better to sit in a coffee shop for an extra two hours before the interview than to show up late, trying to make excuses. Unless unusual circumstances occur, arriving late on an ordinary workday under ordinary circumstances will likely be read by the interviewers as evidence you are a poor planner and lack attention to detail. Explaining that traffic was heavy will probably not gain you much sympathy. In most major cities, traffic is heavy every day, and everyone simply allows for it in their travel time.

Depending on the distance and timing involved for interviews requiring travel to another city or state, you may wish to consider arriving a day early and staying overnight in a nearby hotel, even if the cost is out of your own pocket. This will help ensure you show up the next day to the interview refreshed and on time.

Be sure to check out the logistics of getting to the interview location, whether you will be walking (is rain expected?), taking a cab, automobile (where will you park?), subway, etc. You might telephone someone at the destination well in advance of the interview and inquire about parking and which specific entrance to use. A receptionist or security guard (if applicable) may be a helpful resource and are accustomed to answering such questions.

I recall going to a job interview at a facility located in an unfamiliar complex of office buildings. To prepare, I checked out the destination address online and examined a Google map of the nearby vicinity. Parking options did not seem readily apparent, so I called the office with whom the interview had been arranged. I learned that while on-street parking (coin meters) was available, the odds of finding an open spot at that time of the day were practically nil. The telephone contact suggested a public pay-to-park lot a block away, which was the only real option. Even then, I had to take a chance it would not already be filled to capacity. I also learned that the door of the official street address required an electronic ID pass and was not accessible by visitors. Instead, I needed to enter through a door located on the other side of the block-long building. For security reasons, the visitor entrance had a guard, and I would need to sign in and be escorted to the interview room.

After the telephone call, I located the public parking lot online and planned to use it. The satellite view helped me identify the best walking route from there to the correct building entrance. Fortunately, the weather was predicted to be warm (but not overly hot) and without precipitation, so rain was a non-issue.

You can see where failing to plan and focus on the details could have proven disastrous for my interview. Had I not checked on parking, I might have circled the complex for an hour, never finding an open parking meter and unaware of other available parking options. What if I found a parking lot but coins were required; did I have any? Once at the facility, I certainly would have gone to the wrong entrance, which was locked. Then, after reading the sign, I would have had to walk completely around the block-long building. If inclement weather had been expected and I didn't bring an umbrella, I would have ended up walking the entire distance in the rain. Without proper logistics planning, I could have arrived late, tired, stressed, and soaking wet. Definitely not the best way to show up for a job interview! No matter what I would have said or used as an excuse, the interviewers would have known the real reason was that I failed to plan accordingly.

Still, things can and do go wrong. Suppose you have meticulously planned to ensure on-time arrival, and then the unexpected happens. Perhaps there is a traffic backup on the freeway due to a bad accident, or your flight is delayed and you arrive late. These are matters beyond your control, and while you may have built some extra time into your schedule for minor delays, a two or three-hour delay is probably beyond anything you anticipated. Now what?

As soon as you know what is happening and determine it will result in a delay, call ahead to the office or interview location (whose phone number you should have at the ready). Inform your contact of the situation and the reason, apologize for the inconvenience, and give the expected arrival time (if known). Ask if it would be acceptable to still come or if you must reschedule. If your reason for the delay is reasonable and you call in advance, the employer will likely be understanding and try to accommodate you.

Suppose you arrived on time or, because all went as planned, are even early. Time permitting, this would be an excellent opportunity to visit a nearby restroom and double-check your appearance, hair, clothes, makeup, etc., to ensure nothing unexpected happened along the way.

Your arrival is also when you immediately switch on your "totally professional" mode. It doesn't matter if you are talking to the receptionist, secretary, security guard, or janitor; everyone you meet receives the same level of respect you would give the interviewers. You may not know this, but interviewers frequently ask these first-contact individuals about the demeanor and courtesy of the candidates with whom they interact. Was the applicant friendly? Polite and professional? Your interaction with anyone outside the interview room can be viewed as a candid snapshot of how you *really* conduct yourself.

After all, you are on a job interview and supposedly on your best behavior. If your interaction with these individuals is less than optimal, what will your conduct be like with coworkers, customers, and others once you are hired? You would be surprised how many people put on a great show for the interviewers but treat receptionists, secretaries, and others with less than common courtesy. An unfavorable review from a trusted receptionist or secretary about your attitude and demeanor can cost you the job, regardless of how well you answer questions during the interview. Remember, the interviewers know these people and respect and trust their opinions; they don't know you at all.

GO PREPARED

Ready to go into the interview room? Are you prepared? Always take extra copies of your cover letter and resume. How many? I would recommend no less than three or four of each. This number should satisfy most typical needs unless you have interviews scheduled with multiple individuals or panels at the organization on the same day. If your original application was online, odds are the interviewers will already have copies of your online application, but they may not have the associated attachments. Even if they do, the HR computer system may have rendered these items illegible or unprofessional in appearance. Plus, additional staff members who did not receive copies may join the interview at the last minute.

Applicants will sometimes bring supplemental materials to the interview, including:

- College transcripts
- List of professional references
- Individual letters of recommendation
- Copies of applicable certifications or licenses
- Samples of relevant work

Even though submission of the above items may have been required at the time of application, have extra copies prepared and ready. However, do not bring these out unless they are needed. For example, you might ask the interviewers, "The online application system required me to submit files of my cover letter, resume, list of references, and college transcripts. If you didn't receive these for some reason, I brought additional copies. Is there anything you need?" Even if they do not need anything, this will give the interviewers an opportunity to:

- Confirm to you the various documents came through the online system properly.
- See that you obviously came prepared with extra copies.
- Notice that you are courteous and smart enough to ask.

For materials that may be helpful but were not required at the time of application submission, ask if the interviewers would like to view these. However, be careful not to overload them with papers and documents. Limit the materials to only those most important or relevant; more is not always better. If they would like to see the supplemental items, be sure to indicate which they may keep for later reference, if they wish. Do not ask them to mail anything back to you. If you are going to leave it, consider it disposable. Most interviews are time-constrained, so it is unlikely the interviewers will review every item while you wait.

SHOW AND TELL

Suppose you are a member of an interview panel hiring a photographer for your organization. What is the most obvious factor you need to determine? Most likely, a primary goal would be to learn if an applicant is a talented photographer. You might ask the applicant questions such as:

- What photographic training have you had?
- Would you please describe your work experience as a photographer?
- What brands and types of cameras and other photographic equipment have you used?
- What is your experience and skill level with software such as Adobe Photoshop?

Assuming all your applicants talk a good line and answer the questions favorably, which one do you hire? Despite all the excellent answers, have any of the candidates actually proven their skill or ability? When hiring for a position such as a photographer, a usual requirement is to have each applicant bring a portfolio. By reviewing a portfolio, the interviewers can see examples of the photographer's work and judge its quality for themselves. Admittedly, assessing the quality of any art form, such as photography, is subjective, and the perceived beauty of the work is in the eye of the beholder. However, the point is that the applicant provided tangible work samples to show the interviewers. While presenting a portfolio may be the norm during interviews for photographers, graphic artists, and so forth, how does this apply to your field?

Surprisingly, relatively few candidates bring work samples or other evidence of their skill to an interview. Does your field have something you could show that relates to the position? Every line of work is different, but perhaps it may be appropriate to show:

- Copies of a report or other document you wrote
- Photographs of something you designed or constructed
- Diagrams or schematics
- A small drawing created using AutoCAD
- Charts and graphs you created for a presentation
- A clever or sophisticated spreadsheet you developed
- A website or other online item you created that could be quickly called up on your phone

Of course, *be careful not to show anything that might be considered confidential, sensitive, or proprietary*. This might include documents that include names of individuals, strategic plans, drawings of equipment still under development, and the like. Showing such items suggests an obvious lack of common sense and good judgment on your part. In this situation, your efforts would almost certainly backfire. You might even want to inform the interviewers the materials they are viewing are not confidential, just in case they were wondering.

I once interviewed applicants for an analyst position involving business process improvement (reengineering). The job description clearly indicated applicants must be familiar with flowcharting and process mapping (flowcharting the individual steps of a business process from start to finish). All of the applicants talked about having performed such work, but only two of them brought any samples of their work to demonstrate they had ever actually created a process map. At first, you might think showing samples is unimportant, as it does not necessarily represent proof of skill. It is always possible a candidate could just show a piece of high-quality work created by someone else.

However, by merely asking a few simple but probing questions, it is easy for an interviewer to determine whether the candidate actually created the materials. A deceptive applicant will typically be unfamiliar with the finer details and be hard-pressed to explain precisely how some aspects of the work were accomplished. Yes, plagiarism does sometimes show up during an interview. However, once such candidates are exposed, they accomplish nothing other than proving they lack integrity. They also fail to land the job.

Here's another point. Not only does presenting work samples offer evidence of your skills, but it can also help to favorably *differentiate* you from the other applicants who brought nothing.

INTERVIEW CLASSIFICATION

Suppose all those applications, cover letters, and resumes you submitted have finally paid off, and you have been invited to a job interview. Since there are many different kinds of interviews, you may be wondering what to expect.

What's in a name? Defining interview "formats" and "types" is not an exact science. Different authors use various innovative descriptors for each, and there is no universal agreement on a naming convention. To further muddy the waters, various terms are often used interchangeably.

Here, I will use the following approach to interview classification. For our purposes, the interview "format" will be defined by *the number of interviewers encountered and/or the method or sequence of meeting with them*. Next, there is the "type" of interview. The type will be defined by *the questioning methods or techniques used to acquire information and/or assess the interviewee*.

In reality, regardless of classification, job interviews are often a hybrid mix of formats and types. Employers typically select whatever combination they feel best meets their needs or has worked most effectively for them in the past. Of course, as a candidate, you have no control over this; however, knowing what to expect can help reduce anxiety.

When scheduling an interview, casually ask how it will be conducted. Most employers will likely have no problem providing at least some detail. They might advise whether you will meet with one person or a panel of interviewers. Accept whatever information they offer and don't pry to the point of being annoying or sounding paranoid. Some organizations may post information on their websites about their interviews, such as whether behavioral-based questions (explained later) are used.

INTERVIEW FORMATS

In general, many of the common interview formats you are likely to encounter may include:

- Face-to-Face
- Single Interviewer
- Panel
- Sequential
- Telephone
- Online Video
- Text
- Job Fair
- Meal/Social

Face-to-Face Interview

This is what many might consider the classic, traditional interview format. The candidate meets in-person, face-to-face, with one or more interviewers. For privacy and to avoid noise and distractions, the interview is often conducted in an office or conference room. However, it could just as well take place anywhere, such as on the floor of a factory or at an outdoor job site.

Single Interviewer

With this format, the candidate meets with one individual who conducts the entire interview from start to finish. This may be the business owner, hiring manager, someone from Human Resources (HR), a first-line supervisor, or other person authorized to perform the interview. The individual may make the hiring decision alone or convey their findings to someone who has the power to make the final choice or hiring decision.

Panel Interview

As the name suggests, a panel interview is conducted by several people (often two to five) at the same time. Panel members might consist of the hiring manager and a supervisor but may also include individuals such as a representative from HR, one or more future coworkers, or others.

An interview panel is useful to the employer in many ways. First, the hiring manager receives input from the panel members, who may offer different viewpoints about each candidate. One panel member may notice something which another missed. HR staff are often involved to ensure proper protocol is followed and no illegal questions are asked. Including future coworkers on the panel provides an opportunity for employee engagement in the selection and hiring process. Finally, the use of a panel, especially one with diverse members, may help avoid discrimination or bias, which could potentially occur when only one person conducts the entire interview.

The final hiring decision may be made in several ways:

- One person on the panel (such as a manager) decides with input from the others
- Consensus of panel members
- A vote of the panel
- Someone else (e.g., next level manager) decides based on the recommendation of the panel

During a panel interview, be sure to make eye contact with each person. You never know the relationships, power structure, or group dynamics of the panel, so be careful to treat each member with respect. Panel members often ask questions in a "round-robin" format where each interviewer takes a turn asking questions. Of course, you want to address the person asking the question, but be sure to also make eye contact with the others; not doing so may be perceived as rude or offensive. Otherwise, for example, after you leave the interview room, a member of an all-but-one female panel might comment to the others:

"Did you notice how the candidate mainly looked at and spoke to John through the whole interview? That's probably because John is a man and the candidate assumed the man on the panel was the hiring decision-maker."

Even though you may have had no such belief or ill-intent, this might be the impression you unintentionally leave with the panel.

Sequential Interview

With the sequential format, the interviewee meets with multiple individuals in separate interviews, one after the other. For example, the hiring manager and supervisor may first interview the candidate. Next, the individual is interviewed by a different person, such as a representative from HR. This may be followed by yet another interview, such as someone from another department (Director of Marketing, Finance, etc.), and so forth. Sequential interviews often last several hours or even an entire day. Lengthy sequential interviews are frequently used when hiring for management positions.

In a heavily unionized but progressive work environment, one of the interviews (particularly for management positions) may involve meeting officials from various bargaining units. These union leaders provide input to the hiring party regarding their perceptions of how well a candidate will likely function in an organized labor work environment. The inclusion of union leaders shows good faith on the part of management by actively involving them in hiring decisions that affect their members.

The findings of the separate interviews are later submitted to or discussed with the hiring manager to provide an overall impression of each candidate. This approach is also useful when scheduling conflicts make it difficult to assemble all the needed individuals concurrently for an extended period, such as for a panel interview.

Telephone Interview

As the name indicates, this interview is conducted via telephone. When numerous interviewers are involved, they may be together around a conference table using a speakerphone or located in different offices around the country on a conference call line.

Two of the most important preparations for participating in a telephone interview involve location and technical aspects. Select a location for the call which is private, free from noise and interruption, and has good signal reception (if you are using a cell phone or other portable device). Also, make sure your phone and wireless earbuds are fully charged. The last thing you need is to have this important call terminated early by dead batteries. Nothing says you lack attention to detail like going into a telephone interview with a low battery.

Telephone interviews are frequently used as a low-cost, first-step screening tool (often conducted by HR) when an employer receives numerous applications, or if applicants are widely-dispersed geographically. The screening interviewer may be someone from Human Resources merely reviewing your submission and asking questions to determine more about your actual work experience and education. Other times, someone from the hiring work area may call you for a brief discussion—not a formal interview—just to gain more insight into your background and to hear how you present yourself.

For more detailed information regarding preparation for a telephone interview, see Appendix A: Telephone and Online Video Interviews.

Online Video Interview

When first available, online video interviews were used primarily for screening purposes. These offered an organization the opportunity to preview applicants and decide who to bring in for a "real" face-to-face interview. Online interviews were already commonplace before the COVID-19 pandemic, but became even more so as a result. Today, online video interviews are indeed real interviews. Many individuals go through the entire interview process completely online and are hired without ever having a traditional, in-person interview.

Numerous web-based interview applications are available for these interviews, such as Zoom, Microsoft Skype for Business, Adobe Connect, and GoToMeeting, just to name a very few, with more products always becoming available and companies buying out each other. With some, the interviewee may need to download a small file to their computer in advance (provided by the employer). Other software applications involve the candidate merely clicking a link sent by the employer.

Video has the distinct advantage over telephone interviews of enabling the interviewer(s) to see the candidates and view their reactions to questions, as well as their appearance and mannerisms, and such a format frequently provides an experience quite comparable to that of a physical meeting. Therefore, one must prepare for this interview format accordingly. For example, because the interviewee can be seen, they should wear appropriate attire. Conduct your interview in a private, quiet room where you will not be disturbed (no barking dogs, noisy children, ringing phones, TV in the background, etc.). Anything visible in your background should be clean, appropriate, and non-distracting. Be sure to look at the camera occasionally when speaking, just as you would make eye contact if interviewing in person.

Those few considerations are just the beginning. Because of the technology involved in an online video interview, attention to numerous other details is necessary. For more information, see Appendix A: Telephone and Online Video Interviews.

Text Interview

Although texting has been around in some form for about thirty years, its use as an interview format is relatively new but gaining popularity. Even back in 2014, a Gallup poll found that texting is the most frequently used form of communication among Americans younger than fifty[3]. Additionally, 95% of text messages are read within three minutes of being received[4], making this technology a very fast and efficient way to reach someone. Although text messages are less formal than the traditional phone call or email, human resources staff and search firms have come to recognize texting as yet another viable tool for communicating with and even interviewing job applicants and approaching potential recruits.

When responding to a text message from a known employer or recruiter, always make sure the sender is legitimate and not a phishing scam. Keep in mind that how you respond will likely determine whether you receive any further consideration for employment. Consequently, your text exchange should be professional and not treated in the same manner as your typical, casual chit-chat with friends and family.

- Do not use informal or funny phrase abbreviations such as TY, BTW, LOL, LMK, TTYL, etc.
- Do not use word abbreviations such as "u" for "you," "r" for "are," etc.
- Do not use emojis.
- Autocorrect and text dictation errors can render your otherwise professional-sounding message severely flawed or even obscene. ALWAYS read and double-check the outgoing message before pressing send.
- Even though you may have received this job-related communication through a typically informal and casual method, remember that how you respond is as important as if you were meeting formally and face-to-face.

Job Fair Interview

Colleges, community groups, trade organizations, and even private firms may host job fairs. Job fairs are events specifically designed to bring together job seekers and company recruiters. These may be stand-alone events or held as part of a conference, seminar, or other such meetings. At a typical job fair, applicants walk from table to table with resumes in hand, with each table hosted by a different company. Although these events generally include many employers, individual firms may also hold a job fair exclusively for themselves.

This approach is advantageous and efficient for applicants and employers alike. With a job fair, you can avoid the typical process of "submit a resume to an automated website and hope for a response." This format also provides a company with the opportunity to have a friendly face represent their firm. Presenting a welcoming image may help attract quality applicants who otherwise might have never even heard of the company or bothered to apply. Also, by meeting in person, firms have the chance to see beyond the cookie-cutter, sterile resumes and faceless job applications. This helps them identify candidates with the most potential and insert those applications into the selection process more quickly.

Depending on the job fair, some may recommend you come prepared with a stack of resumes in hand; others may have attendees provide an electronic copy that will be accessible by all participating businesses. While some fairs may be more "meet-and-greet" functions, others may include actual on-the-spot interviews. Even if the interview turns out to be brief and preliminary, it may still open doors.

Finally, if keeping your job search concealed from your current employer is critical, check the job fair website or flyer to see if they are one of the participating companies. More than one job seeker has been shocked after inadvertently walking past their own employer's table and being recognized!

Meal/Social Interview

Interviewers know candidates are guarded and on their best behavior while being formally interviewed. An effective way to get a better glimpse of what a person is really like is to take them to lunch or dinner or place them in some other social situation. The candidate may become more relaxed and reveal more about themselves than they would typically divulge in an interview room. Especially if the job involves wining and dining clients, such as for a sales position, this interview format offers a more realistic view of how an individual might handle themselves in such situations. Do they have good social skills and follow appropriate business and meal etiquette? However, this approach may be used anytime a more revealing look at a candidate is desired for any position.

If invited to such an interview, you have a lot to consider in addition to just the expected job-related questions. Do you know table etiquette? Which entrée should you order—or avoid? Should you have one drink to appear sociable, or none at all?

Interviewers may use alcoholic drinks to loosen the tongues of candidates. What might seem like informal chit-chat to you could be discussion deliberately and specifically intended to get you to reveal negative aspects of yourself which would otherwise remain well-concealed.

Perhaps you know individuals who otherwise routinely appear as solid professionals, but who, when placed in a social but work-related setting involving alcohol, tend to overindulge and act, well, ridiculous. It used to be that such embarrassing conduct was merely the water cooler gossip on Monday morning. Now, thanks to the ever-present smartphone, such individuals are apt to find their uninhibited, party-hardy antics show up in HD-quality video all over social websites within minutes for the entire world to see.

Generally, the safest approach would be that even if your hosts drink during an interview dinner, you should not. By not drinking, there is no chance you will accidentally exceed your limit. This way, there is much less danger of saying or doing something you will later regret. If offered a drink, just politely decline; it is unlikely anyone will question or challenge your decision. However, should the situation really start to feel awkward, or the interviewers appear offended by your refusal, maybe "nurse" one drink, if you are sure you can handle it and it does not lead to additional ones.

Consider the revealing results of a study conducted by researchers from the University of Michigan and the University of Pennsylvania[5]. In a report published in the Journal of Consumer Psychology, the researchers concluded, "Job candidates who ordered wine during an interview held over dinner were viewed as less intelligent and less hireable than candidates who ordered soda." This finding suggests drinking during an interview, even responsibly, might very well backfire.

There are many resources available on the internet regarding proper meal etiquette. I suggest you search for and read several. Regarding silverware, do you know which fork is used for which part of the meal? As you use these utensils, where do you place them? Do you know where to place your cloth napkin during the meal to indicate to the server whether you are finished eating? Do you know why the server may bring you a small dish of sorbet just before your main course? A little advance preparation regarding meal etiquette will not only make you appear a bit more sophisticated, but could possibly save you from embarrassment.

What about your physical eating habits? I recall a dinner business meeting where one individual slurped the soup and chewed their food with an open mouth, all so loudly that the others at the table were shocked and disgusted. Avoid ordering potentially messy foods such as spaghetti or anything with sauces that might drip or splatter. Such entrees might cause you to spend the remainder of the dinner with a big, bright stain on your clothes. Also, go easy on the portion sizes and do not order expensive or unusual foods. No one will be impressed if you order alligator tenderloins as the entrée.

If your interview involves a meal or socializing, never forget you are being watched and scrutinized! Yes, you need to demonstrate you are likable and sociable. However, don't get too comfortable, as your conduct and words will later be discussed and examined under a microscope.

Overlap?

At first, there may appear to be some overlap of formats. Not a problem! No single format seems to fit every possibility. The definition offered earlier permits combinations to clarify the number of interviewers encountered and the method or sequence of meeting them. Consider the two following examples of combinations and see how they can accurately describe an interview:

- Face-to-face single interviewer
- Telephone panel interview

INTERVIEW TYPES

Many different methods or techniques are used to extract information from interviewees and/or assess their potential for success in a job. As with formats, employers frequently mix and combine interview types as needed. The following interview types will be discussed:

- Question and Answer (Q&A)
- Behavioral (STAR)
- Task/Problem Solving
- Skills Tests
- Stress
- Group

Question and Answer (Q&A)

The question-and-answer type probably comes to mind when most people think of a job interview. The interviewer asks the questions, the candidate answers. Simple and straightforward.

The interviewers typically open by asking about the individual's work experience and education. Next, they may pose questions regarding training, skills, or credentials (licenses, certifications, etc.). Especially if the field is technical, a few detailed questions may follow to assess the depth of the candidate's knowledge. At the conclusion of the interview, the candidate usually is offered the opportunity to ask questions of the interviewers.

When preparing for an interview, attempt to anticipate the questions likely to be asked and then develop answers. Typical questions to expect include:

- Tell us about your education and training.
- Tell us about your work experience.
- Are you certified or do you hold a license?
- What computer skills do you possess?
- Describe your experience and skill using [whatever equipment, software, etc. is applicable in your field].
- Why did you apply for this position?
- Where do you want your career to be in five years?
- Why are you the best candidate for this job?

- If offered this position, would you accept it, and why?

This list probably contains no surprises. The internet and interview preparation books are filled with clever, "canned" responses to hundreds of these rather tired, old questions. Don't get me wrong, many of these questions are still valid and relevant, and one can expect at least a few. However, most interviewers today have many other types of questions in their interview arsenal and applicants need to be aware of and prepare for these.

Behavioral (STAR)

Also known as "targeted selection," "situational," "competency-based," or "STAR" (an acronym I'll explain later), the questions asked in a behavioral interview are quite different from those in the typical Q&A type, as they challenge the candidate to recall and elaborate on specific past situations involving certain conduct or behaviors. The underlying premise of this type is that past behavior is a good predictor of future behavior. Applicants may be asked a series of questions such as:

- Describe a time when you had to deal with an irate customer.
- Tell us about a time when you had to complete a project but were not provided adequate resources.
- Tell us about a time when you worked with a team to accomplish a goal.
- Tell us about a time when you worked with people who came from very different backgrounds than yourself.
- Tell us about a time when you had to make an independent decision without consulting your supervisor.

The responses to such questions may provide valuable insight into the way an applicant approaches problems. It can also reveal underlying attitudes about work or people. Candidates tend to be surprisingly honest in their answers, sometimes even exposing very negative aspects of their attitudes or past behavior. Therefore, the behavioral interview type seems to work, at least to some extent, and this may partly explain why it has become so popular. An individual's inability to think of a response may also reveal a lack of sufficient work experience or a general inability to think and respond quickly under pressure.

From experience, I know many candidates awkwardly stumble through such questions and have great difficulty providing a relevant answer. The number one problem I have observed is that individuals are simply not specific enough in their answers. A hypothetical conversation might go like this:

Interviewer: *"Tell us about a time you provided good customer service above and beyond what was normally expected."*

Candidate: *"Uh . . . well . . . um . . . I always provide good customer service to all my clients. I do whatever is needed and help them with resolving any issues. I am a very customer service focused person."*

As you can see, the candidate completely failed to answer the question. The interviewer asked the individual to describe a *specific occasion* when the customer service they provided was *above and beyond* the ordinary. Instead, the candidate provided a vague, general, non-specific answer with no example. After such a response, the interviewer might form the impression the candidate cannot think under pressure or follow directions. Even worse, perhaps the interviewee has no customer service success stories to share!

When answering behavioral questions, consider using the "STAR" approach. STAR is an acronym for Situation, Task, Action, and Result (see next page). In addition to STAR, other similar methods exist, each having its own acronym (e.g., "CAR," referring to Challenge or Context, Action, and Result). However, STAR is very well known and widely used.

The STAR Approach to Answering Behavioral Questions			
S	Situation	Describe the specific situation
T	Task	Describe the task which needed to be accomplished
A	Action	Describe the actions you took
R	Result	Describe the results due to your actions

Had the candidate thought about behavioral questions in advance and considered a situation related to customer service, a much better answer (using the STAR approach) might have gone like this:

Candidate: *"I remember one particular customer who called late, just before we closed at 4 p.m., and due to circumstances beyond their control, they urgently needed a very critical item shipped out ASAP. Unfortunately, our overnight delivery service had already picked up our shipments for that day. I checked our stock and the item was readily available. I could easily fill the order but had to find a way to get it shipped. The overnight shipper has a local terminal and accepts packages until 6 p.m., so I decided to personally drop it off on my way home from work. I assured the client the item would be shipped out the same day. The customer received the needed item the next day, as promised. They were so thrilled and appreciative that they sent a thank-you note to my manager."*

What a difference! This answer cites a very specific example of excellent customer service, provides adequate detail, and yet can be conveyed in less than sixty seconds. If you have no work-related experience upon which to draw for a particular question, some interviewers may accept a non-work example (from college, church, organization, etc.). The interviewer is usually more interested in the *behavior* you exhibited in the situation than *where* it took place.

If you phrase your answers to behavioral questions using the STAR approach, you will hit all the key points the interviewer was hoping to hear. Look at the example just used above; each STAR element was addressed within the answer. Be sure to end on a high note, emphasizing the positive outcome. Unless specifically asked to do so by the interviewer (and some do), you need not announce each element of the STAR as you answer, but phrase your response so each is addressed. If done well, your answer will flow nicely and logically, not sound rehearsed, and yet address each aspect of STAR. Be sure to keep the entire answer brief, as time is usually a limiting factor. If you start to ramble on, the interviewer will lose interest and the potential impact of your response will be diminished.

While some interviewers might use the behavioral interview almost exclusively, many prefer a mix of types, sometimes known as a "blended" interview. This is because behavioral questions can be inherently time-consuming and may not evaluate the specific technical skills needed for a job. For example, for a data analyst position, the employer likely needs to determine a candidate's experience and skill level with software applications such as SAP BusinessObjects and Microsoft Excel. Unless structured to specifically address such work skills, questions regarding soft behaviors alone (teamwork, customer service, honesty, conflict, etc.) would reveal nothing about technical qualifications. However, a technically-oriented behavioral question for a data analyst might be something like, "Describe for us a specific project where you used BusinessObjects to analyze and report enterprise-wide data." Similarly, a machinist might be asked, "Tell us about a time when you faced a particularly challenging setup on a CNC machine." In both examples, the candidates could respond using the STAR method, and their responses would provide insight regarding applicant skill and knowledge.

Since you can reasonably expect to be asked behavioral questions as well as items related directly to your field, you need to prepare for both. Especially with behavioral questions, having answers in mind that can be easily adapted to whatever question you are asked will enable you to be more confident, minimize stress, and help to avoid surprises.

Appendix B contains additional sample behavioral questions. If you are unfamiliar with this format or have not previously encountered it during an interview, you will definitely need to prepare. The pressure of a job interview can make it difficult to readily recall situations of relevance, especially those you would wish to share with a potential employer. Mentally working through behavioral questions in advance will greatly help. Your responses should not sound overly rehearsed, but by considering them ahead of time, you at will at least have some examples in mind upon which you can draw and adapt to the particular question being asked.

Task/Problem Solving

During the interview, you may be given a work-related task to complete or a problem to solve. This approach is very similar to skills testing (see below) but may consist of only one problem or task rather than a broad, perhaps quantitative analysis of your skill sets.

Although the possibilities are endless, here is an example of such a problem: First, the candidate is provided details of a hypothetical work situation, such as an event involving an upset customer or a dispute with another department. Next, the interviewee must draft a response memo within a brief, set amount of time. This exercise provides insight into how the individual would approach a customer service problem, how quickly and effectively the person can think under pressure, and their ability to write professionally.

In some cases, you may be asked in advance to prepare and bring something such as a presentation or document to the interview. If so, make sure it is relevant, well-done, and obviously, your own creation. For example, when hiring for a position where the ability to develop and deliver presentations was essential, I asked each candidate to create, in advance, a ten-minute PowerPoint presentation on an assigned topic and present it during the interview. The most disappointing productions typically contained one or more of the following flaws:

- The presentation was obviously just a plagiarized slideshow, one originally intended for some other purpose and perhaps only minimally related, if at all, to the required topic.
- The individual was so unfamiliar with the presentation content that they read every slide to the interview panel word-for-word. This begs the question of whether or not the candidate actually researched and created the material or simply had poor presentation skills.
- The presentation contained the exact same, easily-Googled, internet-acquired information and graphics as the last two slideshows shown to the panel by other candidates, suggesting a lack of effort or interest.
- The duration of the presentation was either significantly shorter or longer than the specified ten-minute time slot. This demonstrates either a lack of experience or skill in developing and delivering presentations or inadequate rehearsal to fine-tune to comply with the time requirement.

Skills Tests

It is no secret that job applicant skills testing has been around practically forever. Even your grandmother probably took a typing test when she was young and applied for a secretarial position. So, although these have always existed, skills tests previously seemed to be somewhat behind-the-scenes. But as of late, skills testing appears to have become highly visible and more mainstream. For example, television advertisements for popular job search websites now openly tout their services for applicant skills testing. Additionally, there are numerous online testing services available to employers, and many of these have been quietly around for years.

Whether called "pre-employment testing" or "skills tests," their purpose is to help employers get an accurate picture of an applicant's knowledge level in specific areas. Whether the employer wants to know your skill level with spreadsheets, math, customer service, foreign languages, or just about anything else, there is a test available. With this information, employers can quickly process the enormous number of online applications they receive, filtering out all but the most skilled individuals.

Candidates are quick to boast about their skills and abilities in cover letters, applications, and during job interviews. If an employer is looking for someone with a particular skill, every applicant will, of course, claim to have it. Unfortunately, whether done innocently or deliberately, applicants tend to exaggerate their skill levels a bit. After all, everyone wants to look good. Some candidates are real smooth talkers and can be very convincing. Given this, how is an employer to know the actual skill level of each?

Skills tests to the rescue! Applicants can be easily and cost-effectively tested during or after the initial application process. Scores can be automatically calculated and the candidates ranked. Based on those results, a list of perhaps a hundred applicants can be quickly and easily pared down to a more manageable number, such as just the top ten with the highest skill scores.

What does this mean for you? Forewarned is forearmed, so be ready mentally. Skills tests are not always announced in advance. Don't get caught off guard or panic if you encounter a skills test when applying for a position or even during the job interview itself. In fact, you should probably expect one. As more employers now routinely include skills testing as a part of their application and/or interview process, job search websites and other companies have begun to address the needs of the market by offering a broad array of skills testing services.

As an applicant, what should you do to prepare? First, take a close look at the position description or job posting. If it states the need for specific skills, there is your clue. At a minimum, these are the skills you will most likely be asked about during a job interview. However, the employer may do more than just ask or take your word for it. They may test. This could happen any time during the hiring process, from the point of application to the actual job interview.

Next, ask. The fact that you may be required to take a skills test should not be kept a secret. If the job website or communication received from the employer does not mention a skills test, politely ask if there will be one. The employer may even provide helpful information, such as whether the test is technical, a personality test, a math or reading comprehension test, etc.

Finally, prepare for a skills test. Merely being ready for the oral portion of a job interview isn't good enough anymore. Yes, you still need to anticipate the verbal questions you might be asked and have answers ready, but the employer may dig deeper. Are you ready to be tested on those skills you claim to have?

Once you have identified the skills the employer expects, do an honest self-assessment of your proficiency in those areas. If your skills are excellent and up-to-date, great! You are probably good to go! If not, determine the areas which need study and improvement. As mentioned earlier, some fields, such as law enforcement, firefighting, etc., also use physical tests. Can you perform the required number of chin-ups, push-ups, etc. as stated in the description of the physical requirements? If not, you will need to work on these as well.

Fortunately, there are skills testing preparation resources for just about any field. Here are some suggestions for you to investigate:

- Booksellers offer numerous study guides, manuals, and other materials designed specifically for selected government jobs, apprenticeship tests, and various licensure exams.
- Study guides for college placement exams, such as the ACT, SAT, GMAT, and others, have sections covering math, reading comprehension, etc. which are helpful in brushing up your skills. These are readily available from booksellers.
- Many national trade organizations offer study guides for certifications, registries, etc., tailored for their specific fields. If you do not see something listed on their websites, give them a call and ask about available resources.
- Local government, community organizations, or colleges may offer job preparation courses, sometimes at little or no cost.
- Consider taking a college course, either locally or online, for the skill needed.
- Contact a local company or someone working in your career and ask if you could stop in for a brief visit to learn more about the field. They will likely welcome you and may be able to recommend resources.
- Online self-assessment tests are available, but may have a cost. However, before making any purchase, be sure to carefully evaluate the offering to determine its acceptability for your use.

Stress Interview

Certain jobs are high-stress by nature, and not everyone is cut out to work in such a demanding environment. However, some applicants may not be fully aware of the pressure that awaits them once on the job. If so, the employer may be doing themselves and potential employees a favor by evaluating how well job applicants can handle stress.

A college professor related a story to me about a stress interview experienced by a former student. The candidate was given airline tickets to interview in a distant major city. The flight's arrival time was deliberately set (by the employer) for rush hour to cause late arrival to the interview site. The cruelty didn't end there. Once at the designated place, a note was found taped to the meeting room door stating the interview location had been changed to a room in a different building. Again, all done deliberately. After the candidate finally arrived, hopelessly late, the interviewers berated the interviewee for being tardy and angrily demanded an explanation.

Stressed out, sweaty, and exhausted, the candidate could not handle it and fell apart, crying. The interviewers then apologized and explained how every obstacle had been placed there intentionally. They also explained that the situation just experienced was nothing compared to the stress routinely encountered on the job by their employees.

Sure, this is an extreme example of a stress interview. A job interview can sometimes be stressful enough, even without such elaborately contrived hardships. Still, the takeaway here is that, in certain career fields, one might expect the possibility of some type of stress test. No need to be paranoid, but if you are on the lookout, at least you will not be caught off guard. The individual in this example was deliberately set up to fail, with the intent to observe how the stress would be handled. Perhaps a closer review of flight arrangements and expected traffic during travel times might have suggested something was suspicious.

While you are ordinarily unlikely to experience an interview involving such complex, traumatizing measures, your stress tolerance may be tested in other ways. While the approach may be less dramatic, the result can still be very stressful. For example, one or more interviewers may deliberately come across as intimidating or rude, intentionally attempting to provoke you in some way. You may be asked weird questions to throw you off your game. While you cannot anticipate everything that might happen in such an interview, at least knowing (or suspecting) it is all just a deliberate, stress-inducing tactic may help you to remain calm.

Group

With the group interview type, multiple candidates are brought together, often without advance notice, and their reactions and interactions are observed. Even if the interviewers are not yet in the room, the group may be actively observed using video cameras or one-way mirrors. Should you unexpectedly find yourself in this situation, do not visibly react negatively or with panic. Instead, use this as an opportunity to demonstrate how easily you can adapt to any situation and are comfortable functioning in a group.

Often, an exercise may be assigned requiring the individuals to work together to complete it within the allotted time. The interviewers then observe the group dynamics from somewhere in the room or elsewhere, while the candidates work on the task. The session may even be recorded for later review.

The observers watch to see which individuals emerge as natural leaders, how they interact or introduce themselves to each other, and which appear withdrawn or unresponsive. While it is important to speak up during the meeting, do not rudely interrupt others. The interviewers seek both leaders and good team players, not bullies or overly aggressive and pushy people.

Who steps up to cooperatively organize the effort and identify the tasks needed? Which candidates offer helpful suggestions or willingly accept responsibility for critical components of the task? How effective is the communication between team members? Which of the group members demonstrate project management skills?

ANSWERING QUESTIONS

An almost endless selection of books, articles, and internet content exists on the topic of "how to answer interview questions," and you should review some of these resources. Rather than delving into suggested responses to specific questions here, I will offer general guidelines that may help regardless of what questions you encounter.

For efficiency and to accommodate the participants' calendars, employers frequently conduct multiple interviews back-to-back on any one day. These are carefully scheduled, permitting each candidate only a limited amount of time. Therefore, if the interviewers do not inform you, you may wish to ask how much time has been allotted before the interview begins. This way, you can pace yourself accordingly.

I have seen candidates attempt to cram their entire life story into their first answer, which upsets the natural flow of the interview. Answer specifically what is being asked, keeping your responses brief but adequately detailed. Odds are another question will come along, enabling you to elaborate on additional details you would like the interviewers to know. Unless the interviewers ask otherwise, keep your work experience limited to that which is recent and relevant. They do not care that your work history began with a lemonade stand at age ten or that you used some now-obsolete software on a previous job fifteen years ago.

When answering questions, make sure you are talking about *yourself*; i.e., using the first-person singular. Unfortunately, for whatever reason, many individuals seem more comfortable answering questions with "we" sprinkled throughout their responses:

- *"We prepared budget reports for the production staff."*
- *"We developed teaching plans for the classes we taught."*
- *"When patients had minor procedures performed at the bedside, we would prepare the supplies for the physician."*
- *"When customers would call with warranty problems, we had to resolve the issue within 48 hours."*

I recall a colleague who was particularly annoyed by such responses during interviews, and when this occurred, would remind candidates, "I am not hiring '*we*,' I am hiring *you*. Tell us what you did." Whether the candidates realized it or not, they were actually offered excellent advice. The interviewers want to hear about what *you* did personally.

When preparing answers for interview questions, be careful your responses do not sound canned or overly rehearsed. Providing the identical, generic, and safe textbook answer as the last two candidates will not favorably differentiate you. As much as possible, your responses should appear spontaneous and applicable to you personally and the position for which you are applying.

IT'S YOUR TURN TO ASK QUESTIONS

This happens all the time during interviews: Things are going very well so far for the candidate. Then, the interviewers ask, "Do you have any questions for us?" The candidate responds, "Uh... no questions." Really? No questions at all for the interviewers? You are considering quitting your current job to come to work here, and you have zero questions?

Asking no questions whatsoever may signal you are not seriously interested in the job or the field, or, even worse, you are not bright enough to have intelligent questions. The interviewers may be thinking the candidate is not be asking any questions because they:

- Do not have a sufficiently deep level of knowledge regarding this field to even have any intelligent questions.
- Have decided this job is no longer of interest and just want the interview to end.
- Think they already know everything there is to know about this job and the organization.
- Don't really care about this specific job. Maybe the person just wants a job—any job—or is desperately trying to escape their current one.
- Are overly timid, shy, or maybe lack social skills.

Do you really want to leave the interviewers with any of those impressions? Asking no questions—or asking the wrong questions—is a bad way to wrap up an otherwise great interview.

Applicants are often advised to ask typical, canned questions during interviews. For example, "How would you describe the culture at this organization?" Yet, what do you expect them to say? "This is a terrible place to work, look elsewhere"?

No, I recommend avoiding such questions. Put this limited time for questions to work for you. The interviewers are more likely to be impressed by questions that show you took the time to research their organization or if your inquiries are directly related to the position itself. Unless unusual circumstances exist, do not ask more than just a few questions since the interviewers' time is often limited. Here are some hypothetical examples different candidates might ask, and these would, of course, be different for every field:

- *"I saw on CNN and read in Forbes that your company has formed a partnership with XYZ Inc., and the two companies are now sharing complementary fabrication technologies related to 3D printing. I know your company is already an industry leader in implementing 3D printing into its production processes. Do you see this new partnership bringing additional equipment and production capacity to this facility?"*
- *"What do you see as the top three immediate priorities for whomever you hire to fill this position?"*
- *"Does your organization use an enterprise-wide information system? If so, which one, and for what operational functions?"*
- *"Do you have a time frame in which you expect to make a hiring decision?"*

The first question demonstrates the candidate researched the company and is up-to-date on what is currently going on in that industry. The second question is an excellent question for just about any applicant. It shows your interest in learning what your superior and the organization immediately need and expect from you. This question might be particularly applicable when applying for a management position. The third question relates to the information technology in use by the employer. Within your particular field, there may be software commonly used at almost every organization. This question could open the door for interviewers to ask about your skills with such applications if they have not already done so. The last question is very reasonable for anyone and provides useful information for you, but it should not be your only question.

Avoid asking questions so elementary that the interviewers might feel you should already know the answer. You sure don't want them thinking, "Wow. This applicant doesn't even know *that*?"

While you want to learn things about the job to see if it is right for you, watch that your questions do not appear one-sided and focused only on what you will get out of it. Avoid asking questions that might suggest your only actual interest is the salary or some other perk of the job (travel, employee discount, etc.). For example, an applicant once asked only a single question at the end of an interview: "I really like my vacation time. When is the absolute soonest I could take a two-week paid vacation?" Really shows a sincere interest in the job itself, right?

EYE CONTACT MISTAKES

Anyone who has ever received job interview advice has undoubtedly been reminded to maintain good eye contact with the interviewers. Simple advice, but many candidates get it wrong. Here are some common eye contact mistakes to avoid:

- Staring. You do not want to be that applicant who thinks good eye contact means locking eyes with the interviewer and having a no-blink stare-down. Despite what you may have heard, this does not show strength or assertiveness. Aside from the fact it looks unnatural, staring will make you come across as creepy or weird.
- Looking everywhere except at the interviewers. Eye contact advice is given so frequently because many candidates do, in fact, avoid looking directly at the interviewers. They tend to look at the table, the floor, or their papers, but not at the interviewers, perhaps not even realizing what they are doing. Whether true or not, failing to maintain eye contact may be read by interviewers as having weak interpersonal skills or a lack of confidence. You certainly do not want to convey either of those traits! Giving some forethought and practice to possible interview questions and answers can help. You will be more confident, better prepared to answer, and not so apt to unconsciously look away while trying to think of a response.
- Not knowing which interviewer to look at. Often, you will be interviewed by more than one person, perhaps by a panel of four or five individuals. So, which interviewer should you look at? Obviously, when answering, first look at the person asking the question. However, as you continue your response, move your eye contact around

in a natural way to look at the other interviewers as well. The goal is to make each interviewer feel as if you are including them. When ending your answer, look again at the person who asked the question so you can check for visual clues that they understand and are satisfied with your response.

- Trying to focus on the apparent "alpha" interviewer. When answering questions in a panel-type interview, do not try to guess who the real decision-maker is and then focus your eye contact on only them. Not only would that be rude, but you could also pick the wrong person. You have no way of knowing the actual group dynamics or their internal decision process. The final decision-maker may not even be in the room, but might be someone who relies totally on the panel's recommendation. Even if the hiring manager is present, the final selection may be made through group consensus, so offending any interviewer would be a serious mistake.
- Making sexist or other erroneous assumptions about the interviewers. For example, suppose you are being interviewed by three individuals. Two are younger females, and one is an older male dressed in a suit. Some candidates might mistakenly assume the male is the decision-maker, and therefore the one to impress and receive the most eye contact. Don't do it! I have served on many interview panels where I was the only male, dressed in a suit, and the actual decision-maker was a younger but higher-ranking female. The panel will pick up immediately on your mistake and be rightfully offended!
- Making exaggerated eye gestures. Avoid suddenly opening your eyes really wide, such as when you are surprised or startled. Absolutely do not roll your eyes as if disgusted or if you think what somebody said was ridiculous. Eye movements like these might be made unconsciously or out of habit, so stop and consider whether these behaviors are something you might be doing and therefore need to avoid.

SHOULD I NEGOTIATE SALARY DURING THE INTERVIEW?

What about negotiating starting pay and benefits? Should that be done during the interview itself? No, this is not the time to bring it up. Unless your interviewer begins actual salary negotiations, it is best to wait until a position is offered. Think of it this way: When the employer finally decides they want YOU out of all the other applicants, you gain some negotiating leverage. They have invested time and money to find you, and they would not want to lose you over a few dollars.

However, just in case the interviewer happens to offer you a job on the spot and begins negotiating salary, be prepared. See Appendix C: Negotiating a Starting Salary for more detailed information on this subject.

AGEISM AND THE OLDER APPLICANT

Although discrimination against individuals forty years of age or older (ageism) has been illegal since 1967, it still widely exists and is openly practiced. According to the U.S. Equal Employment Opportunity Commission (EEOC), "Unfounded assumptions about age and ability continue to drive age discrimination in the workplace," and "age discrimination remains a significant and costly problem for workers, their families, and our economy."[6]

If you are an older (no, make that "experienced" or "seasoned") applicant, this form of discrimination is yet another obstacle you will face and need to overcome when seeking employment. At first, ageism may seem counterintuitive. Should not an employer value and welcome a highly-experienced applicant who has spent years developing their skills and knowledge? Unfortunately, those gray hairs may trigger a totally different response. When encountering a seasoned candidate, an interviewer may wonder:

- Is this individual physically up for the job?
- Does this person have health problems that will lead to frequent absences?
- Is the worker "set in their ways" and unable to adapt to our way of doing things?
- How would this older individual handle reporting to a much younger supervisor?
- My grandmother and grandfather cannot use a computer or smartphone. How tech-savvy is this person?
- Is this older worker "on autopilot" and "just skating by" with minimal effort until retirement?

- We will invest considerable time and training in this person. How long will they actually stay here and be productive?

That is just the tip of the iceberg. Although the EEOC report cited above may consider these "unfounded assumptions about age and ability," experienced candidates encounter such biases all the time. If you are in that age demographic, accept that whether it is legal or not, you, too, will likely face age discrimination. What can you do to help overcome it?

Attempting to completely conceal your age is probably impossible. Besides, your efforts to do so will ultimately become obvious and make you appear deceptive. Plus, stereotypes about age are already out there, and you cannot erase them from people's minds. Perhaps a more reasonable approach is to take measures that tend to deemphasize your age. This may be done by removing from your application materials, online presence, and personal appearance anything that might tend to feed those negative age stereotypes. For example:

- On your resume, do not include dates of college degrees or training courses.
- List only your most recent employment. If you have worked at the same firm for many years and held various positions, show only your most current position or promotion.
- Having no online presence at all could suggest you are either pretty old, not very good with technology, or hiding something. At minimum, create a LinkedIn account or update your current one. If you use a profile photo, make it a professional and distinguished-looking image such as you would see on a corporate website. If you have a Facebook account, it may already contain plenty of clues about your age (discussions about grandkids, recent surgeries, lots of older friends, etc.). Additionally, there may be a few not-so-flattering posts you might not want a potential employer to see. In fact, it might be a good idea, at least temporarily, to change your account privacy settings. If any social media sites currently permit the public to view your content, adjust the settings so only friends can see anything. This way, an employer who checks you out online will only find your professional-looking LinkedIn page—and that is something you can control.
- Numerous find-a-person type websites exist that may list you and show your age, and these are often filled with errors. Do an online search for your name and see what shows up. Some sites may allow you to request corrections or to be removed.
- Does your hairstyle (or beard) reflect a modern, professional appearance?
- Does your interview attire appear dated? Check the biographies or other photos on the website of your potential employer and see what current employees are wearing. However, do not dress inappropriately for your age or else you will merely look ridiculous.
- This one is really hard . . . If necessary, and if time permits, is there anything you can do to enhance your physical appearance by losing weight, getting in shape, etc.? Your pace and body movements should suggest you are energetic. Huffing and puffing at the interview after walking only a short distance will not help your cause.
- Maintaining good eye contact will help convey alertness and focus. Practicing and rehearsing answers in advance of an interview will enable quick responses, projecting mental sharpness.

Emphasize the extensive experience you bring to the table. Indicate how you readily adapt to new procedures or software. As evidence of your dependability, work into the conversation how you received perfect attendance awards from your current employer, but only if it is true.

Again, you cannot control what stereotypes regarding age others may carry around in their heads. However, you can avoid accidentally reinforcing or validating such perceptions. If you do not fit an interviewer's preconceived notion of an "old person," you are less apt to be considered one.

YOUR PERSONAL READINESS: INTERVIEWING

- ➤ When preparing to attend an in-person interview, have you considered the following?
    - o Travel logistics
    - o Allowing adequate travel time
    - o Parking or other transportation considerations
    - o Proper dress for weather at the destination
    - o Contact information in the event you must report a delay
    - o Inquiring about the interview format or type
- ➤ Do you have extra copies of any needed materials, such as cover letters, resumes, college transcripts, etc.?
- ➤ Do you have samples of your work, if applicable?
- ➤ If participating in a telephone or online video interview, have you made adequate preparations?
- ➤ Is a skills test likely? If so, have you prepared?
- ➤ Have you tried to anticipate verbal interview questions, both general and job-specific, and have answers ready?
- ➤ Have you tried to anticipate behavioral-type questions and have adaptable examples ready?
- ➤ Are you familiar with the STAR format of answering behavioral questions?
- ➤ Do you have questions prepared to ask the interviewers?
- ➤ If you are a seasoned applicant, have you taken steps to deemphasize your age?

Interviewing (Part 3): After the Interview

Once the interview is over, you might assume the interview readiness factor is no longer relevant. Not true! A few tasks still await you.

DEBRIEF

After a military operation, soldiers are debriefed to determine how things went during the mission and to identify any unexpected problems they may have encountered. The information gathered provides valuable insight regarding enemy tactics and enables more effective planning for future missions. The first thing you should do after an interview is to debrief yourself.

Once you are somewhere where you can take a break, do so, and mentally replay what just occurred. Do this immediately while every aspect of the interview is still fresh in your mind, and *make written notes* for future reference.

- Did anything happen during the interview that caught you off guard?
- What questions were you asked?
- Were there any questions you found particularly difficult to answer?
- If you could go back in time and repeat the interview, what would you do differently?

Often, it may be a while before you find out whether you got the job. Making detailed notes right away will help ensure the knowledge and insight gained from this experience is retained and available for use for next time, if needed.

THANK THE INTERVIEWERS

Should you send a follow-up "thank-you" after the interview? For years, the interview etiquette norm was that candidates were expected to mail a polite letter to each interviewer, thanking them for the interview. Opinions are mixed on whether such expressions of gratitude directly influence the actual hiring decision, as some interviewers expect them, while others do not. Besides, physical cards or letters often arrive well after the hiring decision has been already made, so why bother? Is sending some type of thank-you message rather "old school" and merely an outdated tradition from a bygone era? Not really.

Good manners never go out of style, and sending a polite note serves to confirm your professionalism. It also helps to leave a positive impression of you for next time, should you be asked in for a second interview or wish to pursue other employment with the same organization in the future. Additionally, your competitors may have sent thank-you notes, and you do not want them looking better than you! Besides, you have nothing to lose:

- If the interviewer thinks applicants should send thank-you notes, you will have met the expectation.
- If the interviewer does not care either way about thank-you notes, nothing was lost.

Since electronic communication is so commonly accepted in business, easy and fast compared to traditional "snail mail," and contact information is often readily available, sending a brief email of appreciation shortly after the interview should be a simple matter. At some point near the end of the interview, simply ask the interviewers for their business cards. These will provide you with the correct spelling of their names, titles, and email addresses. If the interviewers did not have cards available, ask for this information afterward from a receptionist or secretary. You may also find the needed information on the company website. However, that approach should be a last resort, as email addresses are sometimes intentionally left off such sites. The follow-up communication should be brief and to the point; simply prepare a message conveying that:

- You sincerely appreciated being granted an interview.
- You enjoyed meeting the interviewers and discussing the position.
- The interview reinforced your interest in the job.
- You would very much like the opportunity to join the organization.

Keep your communication short and simple. A lengthy dissertation regarding all the merits of hiring you and explaining why you are the best candidate will likely not help at this point. You had your chance during the interview. This thank-you message should also be written as carefully and professionally as your other application and interview materials. A poorly worded email at this point will only serve to diminish any favorable impression you may have made.

WHAT IF YOU DIDN'T GET THE JOB?

Oh no! Suppose you find out you did not get that particular position. Now what? Your initial reaction might be depression ("I don't know why I even thought I had a chance at getting that job!") or even anger ("I didn't want to work for those losers anyway!"). Such emotions, while perhaps natural, are not productive. Instead, approach the situation as follows:

- Accept that not every job interview will result in an offer.
- Think of each interview as a learning experience and good practice for the future.
- Review your post-interview debriefing notes again and reassess the quality of the responses you gave during the interview. Then, prepare for next time.
- Contact the interviewer(s) and politely ask for constructive feedback; some may be willing to provide it.

Above all, don't despair or give up! Not everyone aces an interview the first time, especially if it has been a while since you last interviewed or this was your first serious job interview. It may take a few tries to hone your interview readiness skills, raise your confidence level, and reduce the stress that may have hampered your performance.

Also, you may not have actually done anything wrong during the interview. It is always possible you were simply up against very strong competition from more experienced or better-qualified candidates. It happens. In addition, the employer may have had issues about which you were not aware, unrelated to your performance. For example, there might have been a last-minute hiring freeze, the position may have been eliminated due to an internal reorganization before it could be filled, or perhaps there was an internal HR issue requiring the hiring of an inside candidate. You would likely never hear about such problems, and even if you did, they are issues outside of your control.

However, if you recall stumbling around for an answer to a reasonable question during the interview, consider how you could answer it better in the future. Do you need to brush up on something? Were you asked a behavioral question which you had not anticipated?

After learning they have lost out on a job, it rarely occurs to most candidates to contact one or more of the interviewers and politely ask for constructive feedback. If you really intend to ask for such feedback, keep in mind the following:

- Be respectful and positive.
- You must be mentally prepared and receptive to constructive criticism and able to listen to it silently without becoming angry or trying to interject defensive comments into the conversation. Accept that the decision has already been made. There is absolutely no point now in elaborating on the answers you gave or explaining why

you did this or that. If you can't have such a sensitive conversation without getting defensive, then don't bother. You will only do more damage than good, especially if you intend to pursue a future opening with that organization.

- Don't try to drill down for every tiny detail; the conversation will likely be limited to somewhat general terms. Most interviewers will not share their private discussions with interview panel members or reveal specific details of why you were not hired.
- Many interviewers may, at first, be somewhat hesitant to provide any feedback at all. They may be uncomfortable having such a conversation or fear you might be "fishing" for something which could be construed as bias or even illegal discrimination. The sad fact is, we live and work in a very litigious society. People can and do make claims and file lawsuits, whether valid or not, that can create significant problems. You may need to convince the interviewer through the tone of your request that your intentions are honorable and you are genuinely only looking to see where you can improve your interviewing skills.
- If you are provided feedback, even if you disagree with it, politely thank the interviewer for their time and willingness to speak with you. If you believe their comments are invalid, you will need to do some serious soul-searching to determine whether the problem is with them, or with you—and if, perhaps, you really do need to change something.
- If you have been unsuccessful at several interviews and received similar feedback each time, consider the old adage: "Insanity is doing the same thing over and over and expecting different results."

Receiving interview feedback and learning from it can be one of the most valuable resources available to you for improving your interviewing readiness factor.

Self-Assessment of the Readiness Factors

The previous chapters explored the six readiness factors in detail. While reading, you may have started to wonder about your own level of preparedness. In this chapter, you will perform a self-assessment to determine exactly that—your personal level of readiness regarding each of the six factors. The self-assessment tools that follow are specific for each factor. Answer the questions objectively and with complete honesty.

"The first principle is that you must not fool yourself—and you are the easiest person to fool."

- Richard Feynman

What if you are not ready with respect to each factor? Does that mean you should not even bother to apply for a job at this time? No, because the factors are not necessarily pass/fail in nature. Think of them more as degrees of readiness. Of course, the more prepared you are with each factor, the more likely you are to succeed.

Different career fields and employers all place varying emphasis on each of the factors. For example, as discussed previously, some fields absolutely require a license. Without one, you have no chance whatsoever of securing a job. Yet, in other fields, the credential readiness factor may play little or no role at all. Still other careers require full and extensive preparation with every factor.

The self-assessment tools may reveal that, for some factors, you are not adequately prepared. If so, the Individual Development Plan (IDP), which you will complete in the next chapter, is designed to establish a logical course of action to ensure you will become ready.

EDUCATION SELF-ASSESSMENT

The education self-assessment tool utilizes a series of yes/no responses to a set of questions. At first, assessing your readiness regarding education might seem unnecessary. After all, isn't the real question simply whether or not you have the required education or training? While this is probably true in many cases, some career fields are very specific as to the degree level, type, and accreditation required. Have you considered all these critical details?

The self-assessment tools use a step-by-step approach to help ensure you ask all the right questions and methodically think through each factor. The tools for the remaining factors are similar in concept. The following example will walk you through the first tool.

Naomi, who is currently working in a dead-end, minimum-wage position, has decided to pursue a career in real estate sales. She researched the field and learned that, although there is no college degree requirement in her particular state, obtaining a state-issued real estate license will be mandatory to work in that field. Naomi checked the state licensing website and spoke with a few real estate brokers for more detailed information. She learned that before applying to take the state license examination, she must first complete specific pre-licensing courses. Using the self-assessment tool, Naomi circled her responses.

As she had already diligently researched the educational requirements to enter the real estate field, Naomi responded "Yes" to the first question. It is important to ensure that when performing such research, you use official sources (such as the state licensing website in this example) as well as multiple other reliable sources. Speaking with several professionals is very helpful, but keep in mind the educational requirements may have changed since they first entered the field.

Additionally, be sure to check multiple current job postings to determine the type and extent of education or training currently being expected of applicants. Failure to perform this detailed research could result in a waste of time and money spent obtaining education or training that was unnecessary or did not meet the specific requirements.

Education/Training Readiness Self-Assessment

#	Question	Yes	No
1.	Have I researched the education and training requirements for my chosen career field?	Yes (Continue to #2)	No *Not Ready* (Go to IDP)
2.	Does my career require a minimum of a high school diploma or equivalent?	Yes (Continue to #3)	No (Go to #9)
3.	Do I have a high school diploma or equivalent?	Yes (Continue to #4)	No *Not Ready* (Go to IDP)
4.	Does my career require education or training beyond a high school diploma or equivalent?	Yes (Continue to #5)	No **READY**
5.	Is a college degree required for my career field?	Yes (Continue to #6)	No (Continue to #9)
6.	Do I have a degree in the required major or acceptable alternative, and is it of the required level (associate, bachelor, etc.)?	Yes (Continue to #7)	No *Not Ready* (Go to IDP)
7.	Does the career field require the college and/or degree program to meet specific accreditation requirements?	Yes (Continue to #8)	No (Go to #9)
8.	Does my college and/or degree program meet all specific accreditation requirements?	Yes (Continue to #9)	No *Not Ready* (Go to IDP)
9.	Is specialized training required for my career field?	Yes (Continue to #10)	No **READY**
10.	Have I completed the required training?	Yes **READY**	No *Not Ready* (Go to IDP)

Naomi moved on to Question 2 and responded "Yes," as a high school diploma or equivalent is a prerequisite in her state for taking the required training classes. She graduated from high school, so she answered "Yes" to Question 3. Next, she indicated "Yes" to Question 4, as she knows from her research that real estate pre-licensing training courses are required.

Since a college degree is not required in her state, Naomi answered "No" to Question 5. The "No" response instructed her to continue to Question 9. As training courses are required in her state before she can apply to take the license exam, a "Yes" answer was given to Question 9. Since she has not yet completed the real estate courses, Naomi answered "No" to Question 10.

The self-assessment concludes Naomi is not yet prepared regarding the education readiness factor. However, creating an individual development plan will help her develop a course of action to become ready. Her IDP will involve tasks such as researching the availability of such classes, registering for the courses, and completing the necessary pre-licensing instruction. Now complete the education self-assessment for yourself.

Self-Assessment of the Readiness Factors

Education/Training Readiness Self-Assessment

1.	Have I researched the education and training requirements for my chosen career field?	Yes (Continue to #2)	No **Not Ready** (Go to IDP)
2.	Does my career require a minimum of a high school diploma or equivalent?	Yes (Continue to #3)	No (Go to #9)
3.	Do I have a high school diploma or equivalent?	Yes (Continue to #4)	No **Not Ready** (Go to IDP)
4.	Does my career require education or training beyond a high school diploma or equivalent?	Yes (Continue to #5)	No **READY**
5.	Is a college degree required for my career field?	Yes (Continue to #6)	No (Continue to #9)
6.	Do I have a degree in the required major or acceptable alternative, and is it of the required level (associate, bachelor, etc.)?	Yes (Continue to #7)	No **Not Ready** (Go to IDP)
7.	Does the career field require the college and/or degree program to meet specific accreditation requirements?	Yes (Continue to #8)	No (Go to #9)
8.	Does my college and/or degree program meet all specific accreditation requirements?	Yes (Continue to #9)	No **Not Ready** (Go to IDP)
9.	Is specialized training required for my career field?	Yes (Continue to #10)	No **READY**
10.	Have I completed the required training?	Yes **READY**	No **Not Ready** (Go to IDP)

EXPERIENCE SELF-ASSESSMENT

The experience self-assessment tool format is similar to that used for education. Read each question and answer honestly and objectively.

Experience Readiness Self-Assessment		
1. Have I researched the amount and type of work experience employers are currently requiring for a position in my chosen career field?	Yes (Continue to #2)	No **Not Ready** (Go to IDP)
2. Is a minimum amount or type of experience required?	Yes (Continue to #3)	No **Ready**
3. Do I have the required minimum amount and type of work experience?	Yes **Ready**	No (See Note A) (Continue to #4)
4. Is it possible to obtain the required experience in my present job or with my present employer?	Yes (Continue to #5)	No **Not Ready** (See Note B)
5. Have I approached my employer to request opportunities to gain the necessary experience?	Yes **Not Ready** (Go to IDP; gain experience until ready)	No **Not Ready** (Discuss with employer)

Note A: Unless prohibited by law, some employers will consider hiring applicants who have less than the normally required amount of experience. If true in your situation, consider applying for positions using whatever experience you currently possess. Continue to Question #4.

Note B: If experience is mandatory for entry into the desired career and your current employer or position is not able to provide any opportunities to gain such experience, you may need to consider:
- Identifying experience you may have with organizations outside of work (volunteer, church, community service, etc.) that may serve as an acceptable substitute.
- Switching to a trainee or entry-level position in the desired field with your current employer, if one exists, to gain experience. Such positions often require less or no experience.
- Seeking employment with another employer who can provide a position or opportunities to gain experience.

SKILLS SELF-ASSESSMENT

The type and number of skill sets expected by employers vary considerably by field, position, and employer. However, as discussed previously, good interpersonal and communication skills are also applicable and necessary regardless of the field, position, or employer. Without these, you will probably not get hired in the first place, and even if you do, you will likely not go far. Complete the skills self-assessment.

	Skills Readiness Self-Assessment		
1.	Have I researched and identified the various skills and abilities currently required by employers in my career field? These may include, but are not limited to, the following: • Technical • Specific Software • Math • Use of Tools • Use of Equipment • Negotiating • Clinical • Physical Abilities • Computer • Leadership • Public Speaking • Sales • Teaching • Troubleshooting • Art/Graphics • Engineering • Trade-Related • Data Analysis	Yes (Continue to #2)	No ***Not Ready*** (Go to IDP)
2.	Am I currently competent in each of the skills and abilities identified as necessary by my research?	Yes (Continue to #3)	No (Go to IDP)
3.	Good interpersonal skills are important for any position or career field. On a scale of 1 (poor) to 10 (excellent), using whole numbers only, I would rate my current interpersonal skill level as:	Score 8 to 10 (Continue to #4)	Score 1 to 7 ***Not Ready*** (Go to IDP)
4.	Are good writing skills critical or important in my desired career field?	Yes (Continue to #5)	No ***Ready***
5.	On a scale of 1 (poor) to 10 (excellent), using whole numbers only, I would rate my current writing skill level as:	Score 8 to 10 ***Ready***	Score 1 to 7 ***Not Ready*** (Go to IDP)

CREDENTIALS SELF-ASSESSMENT

The types of credentials applicants must possess vary considerably by field, position, employer, and geographic location (state, county, city, township, etc.). Complete the credentials self-assessment.

Credentials Readiness Self-Assessment		
1. Have I researched whether credentials (certifications, licenses, etc.) are currently applicable in my desired career field and in the geographical area in which I intend to work?	Yes (Continue to #2)	No **Not Ready** (Go to IDP)
2. Are specific credentials currently required by employers and/or law?	Yes (Continue to #3)	No **Ready** (See Note A)
3. Will it be mandatory to have the credentials at the time of hire?	Yes (Continue to #4)	No (See Note B) (Continue to #4)
4. Do I currently possess each of the required credentials?	Yes **Ready**	No **Not Ready** (Go to IDP)
Note A: Even if not specifically required by law or the employer, possession of applicable credentials might be a favorable differentiating factor. Note B: If a particular credential is not mandatory at the time of hire, you may be ready now. However, if obtaining the credential will be a condition of continued employment, be sure to include the necessary preparation in your individual development plan (IDP). Under these circumstances, failure to acquire the required credential within the allowed period of time may result in termination of your employment.		

DIFFERENTIATION SELF-ASSESSMENT

In this self-assessment, you will examine yourself objectively from the viewpoint of the employer. When compared to others who may apply for the position, what makes you stand out favorably? Or, would you just be another clone candidate who meets the bare minimum requirements? In other words, why should the employer hire you instead of another candidate? What makes you the more desirable candidate?

When using this tool, you will provide two answers to each question. The first response (Yes or No) answers the question itself, such as whether or not you have a work-related credential (license, certification, etc.). The second response (Yes or No) indicates whether the question applies to your field or situation. For example, if your particular field does not have any applicable credentials, the response would be "No."

After answering the questions, add the number of "Yes" responses in the "My Answer" column and enter the total in Box A. Next, add the number of "Yes" responses in the "Question Applicable?" column and enter the total in Box B. Finally, divide A by B and multiply by 100. The result indicates a relative readiness score (as a percentage) regarding differentiation.

Differentiation readiness is a matter of degree, and there is no clearly defined, acceptable "Ready" score. However, if your score is 0% or very low, consider taking steps to favorably distinguish yourself from other similarly qualified applicants. It is unlikely any candidate possesses every differentiating quality shown in the tool, as some questions refer to items that may be very difficult or expensive to attain. The goal is to identify and achieve those differentiating factors which are *reasonable for you*.

Differentiation Readiness Self-Assessment

#	Question	My Answer		Question Applicable?	
1.	I have education (or non-degree training, if the norm in my field) beyond the minimum required or expected of applicants for this position.	Yes	No	Yes	No
2.	I have significantly more or higher-quality work experience than the minimum required or expected of applicants for this position.	Yes	No	Yes	No
3.	I have work-related skills in addition to the minimum required or expected.	Yes	No	Yes	No
4.	I have a work-related credential (license, certification, etc.) when none is specifically required or expected; or, I have more credentials than the minimum required or likely to be possessed by other applicants.	Yes	No	Yes	No
5.	I have active memberships in one or more work-related organizations or professional associations which are well-known and respected in my field.	Yes	No	Yes	No
6.	I read current and recognized work-related trade journals or magazines and am knowledgeable about recent topics, trends, or issues in my field.	Yes	No	Yes	No
7.	I have attended recent, work-related conferences or seminars conducted by established, recognized organizations or professional associations in my field.	Yes	No	Yes	No
8.	I am building a professional network and am personally known by one or more individuals working for potential employers.	Yes	No	Yes	No

Differentiation Readiness Self-Assessment (Continued)

		My Answer		Question Applicable?	
9.	I have, on my own initiative, participated in programs, activities, classes, etc. intended to promote my professional development. These were not required by my employer or mandated for licensure or certification.	Yes	No	Yes	No
10.	I am actively involved (beyond just donating money) in volunteering with community or charitable organizations, their fundraisers and benefits, and other similar activities.	Yes	No	Yes	No
11.	I have other attributes, achievements, etc. which will differentiate me favorably from other candidates. These include: _____ _____ _____ _____	Yes	No	Yes	No
Count the number of "Yes" responses in the "My Answer" and "Question Applicable" columns and enter the totals for each.		**Totals:**		A _____	B _____
Divide A by B and multiply by 100 to obtain the percentage score for differentiation readiness. (A/B x 100)		**Readiness Score:**		_____ %	
Note: Differentiation readiness is a matter of degree. There is no clearly defined acceptable "Ready" score. It is unlikely any candidate possesses every differentiating attribute above. However, if your score is 0% or very low, consider taking reasonable steps to favorably distinguish yourself from other similarly qualified applicants.					

INTERVIEWING SELF-ASSESSMENT

This self-assessment will examine your degree of readiness to participate in a job interview. This tool consists of two parts; the first is a general readiness assessment, and the second should also be used if you have an actual job interview scheduled.

Ideally, readiness for this factor should be at 100%. However, interview readiness is also a matter of degree. The more you prepare, the more likely an interview will be successful.

Evaluate your readiness objectively and then decide your satisfaction level with the results. Any items not answered "Yes" should be considered for inclusion in your individual development plan.

Interviewing Readiness Self-Assessment
PART 1 – Basic Readiness

1.	I can clearly and concisely describe my education and training and have practiced giving responses aloud.	Yes	No
2.	I can clearly and concisely describe my work experience and have practiced giving responses aloud.	Yes	No
3.	I can clearly and concisely describe my applicable skills and have practiced giving responses aloud.	Yes	No
4.	I have attempted to anticipate possible work-related questions (e.g., technical, clinical, procedural) likely to be asked and have practiced my responses.	Yes	No
5.	I can speak knowledgeably about regulations, laws, codes of ethics, standards, safety, etc. that apply to my field.	Yes	No
6.	I have reviewed numerous typical generic interview questions, developed responses, and practiced answering aloud.	Yes	No
7.	I have reviewed numerous behavioral interview questions and recalled my own related experiences. I am prepared to call upon these experiences to answer such questions using the STAR approach and have practiced responses aloud.	Yes	No
8.	I can speak knowledgeably about my experience, competency, and skill relating to computers, software, and technology, including social media, if applicable.	Yes	No
9.	If an interview involves a skills test or actual demonstration of proficiency (e.g., physical skills, use of specific software, equipment, etc.), I am prepared.	Yes	No
10.	I have objectively evaluated my interpersonal skills (e.g., eye contact, speaking voice, habits, etc.) and have attempted to improve these where necessary.	Yes	No
11.	My resume, CV (if applicable), and list of professional references are up-to-date and ATS friendly.	Yes	No
12.	I am thoroughly familiar with the contents of my resume and other materials and can accurately discuss them with ease and without continually needing to look at the documents.	Yes	No
13.	I have unofficial copies of my college (or high school) transcripts and know the process of sending an official copy if requested.	Yes	No
14.	My social media and other online presence reflect me in a positive and professional manner.	Yes	No
Count the total number of "Yes" responses.		**Total:**	_____
Divide the total by 14 and then multiply by 100 to obtain the percentage score for interview readiness. (Total/14 x 100)		**Readiness Score:**	_____

Interviewing Readiness Self-Assessment **PART 2 – Interview is Scheduled**			
1.	I have inquired as to the expected interview format (e.g., face-to-face, single/panel, online, etc.).	Yes	No
2.	If a physical interview, I have worked out the logistics and addressed other applicable details, including: • Address and travel route • Travel time required, allowing for extra time • Transportation modes to use • Parking location • Building entrance and where to check in • Contact name and telephone number in case of a delay • Copies of my resume or CV, cover letter, credentials, references, transcripts, examples of work, and other such materials have been prepared	Yes	No or N/A
3.	If a telephone or online video interview, I have prepared by: • Charging any required battery-operated devices • Selecting a private and quiet location • Considering the requirements of the technology and software • Determining the best lighting and camera position for video	Yes	No or N/A
4.	I am familiar with the job description for the position.	Yes	No
5.	I have developed and rehearsed answers and talking points for questions I may be asked.	Yes	No
6.	I have researched the employer's organization.	Yes	No
7.	I have developed and rehearsed the questions I will ask the interviewers.	Yes	No
8.	I have researched competitive salary levels for this position in the geographical location, made my decisions regarding what constitutes acceptable compensation, and developed and rehearsed negotiation talking points.	Yes	No
Count the total number of "Yes" responses.		**Total:**	
Divide the total by 7 and then multiply by 100 to obtain the percentage score for scheduled interview readiness. (Total/7 x 100) Note: A denominator of 7 is used as questions 2 and 3 are mutually exclusive.		**Readiness Score:**	

After completing the self-assessment for each readiness factor, proceed to the next chapter. There, you will create an individual development plan designed to enhance your readiness for any factors identified as needing improvement.

Creating Your Individual Development Plan (IDP)

In the previous chapter, you assessed your preparedness relative to each of the six readiness factors. It is likely you concluded additional preparation is necessary for some or even all the factors. While completing the forms, you may have even been thinking about what steps you should take to enhance readiness in areas that may need improvement. In this chapter, you will organize those thoughts by writing down the goals, along with the action steps necessary. These goals and the required actions make up a strategic plan for your personal development, often referred to as an Individual Development Plan (IDP).

The IDP concept is not new. The human resources departments of many organizations have used various types of IDPs to support employee development for years. In fact, some have adopted a formal approach, requiring all employees to work with their managers to develop such plans.

DEVELOPING "SMART" GOALS FOR YOUR IDP

In the 1980s, the "SMART" goal-setting concept was introduced. Because it is a simple and common-sense approach, it remains popular even today, and organizations often modify it to fit their individual needs. SMART is an acronym for **S**pecific, **M**easurable, **A**ttainable, **R**elevant, and **T**ime-Based, all attributes of properly developed goals.

		SMART Goals
S	Specific	The identified goal must be very specific in nature. Generic statements, such as "I will gain additional experience," are not acceptable. A specific goal might be, "To gain experience, I will manage three organization-wide IT projects involving the transition from server-based applications to cloud-based applications."
M	Measurable	A goal must be measurable. Otherwise, how do you determine the progress made toward attainment or know when it has been achieved?
A	Attainable	A goal may be well-intended but unattainable. An unrealistic goal contributes nothing to the plan and only serves to discourage and frustrate the planner. Goals do not have to be easy, but they do have to be *attainable*. At this time, also consider what, if any, additional resources you may need to ensure the goal can be reached. These might include funding, assistance from others, allocation of extra time, etc.
R	Relevant	Every goal must contribute directly toward the completion of your overall career plan. If it does not, then it merely consumes valuable energy and resources without contributing toward the desired results. If a particular goal does not contribute directly, then it should not be included in your plan.
T	Time-Based	Goals that are not time-based are usually put off until "someday," a date which typically never comes. Assigning a specific deadline by which to meet the goal will give you a target, help you determine whether you are on track along the way, and aid you in creating a self-imposed sense of urgency. An endpoint or deadline date must be included, but lengthy goals should be divided into a series of smaller "milestone" targets (with dates) as you move along the path toward completion.

As you move forward and create your IDP, it is important to ensure each individual goal or task in the overall plan is SMART in nature. The individual elements of SMART will vary in applicability from goal to goal. Some will be completely obvious, whereas others may require more thought.

The IDP templates were designed to help incorporate the SMART elements. Many of the templates have a format similar to the self-assessment tools used previously. However, whereas the assessment tools used earlier were designed to ask "Have I?" the IDP templates follow up with the development of "How I will" steps. Space on each page may be limited, so when developing your IDP, feel free to use additional sheets of paper as needed to document your findings or expand on the actions required.

MILITARY RESOURCES

When developing your IDPs, you may want to consider service in the armed forces as a potential resource applicable to several readiness factors. For example, the military can provide education and training, hands-on experience, and skills transferable to the civilian workforce, along with benefits to assist with college tuition. Many have found that serving their country opened the door to a successful career later or even became a career path of its own.

Some branches of the military may have programs whereby a recruit is guaranteed training in a specific field or specialty before actually enlisting. Such programs are quite competitive, openings may be limited, and candidates must meet certain eligibility requirements. As the specifics regarding these programs vary and are subject to change, they will not be discussed here. Interested individuals are encouraged to discuss these programs directly with the branch of interest to learn the full details.

INDIVIDUAL DEVELOPMENT PLAN FOR EDUCATION/TRAINING

	Individual Development Plan for Education/Training		
1.	Did the self-assessment indicate I am ready regarding the education readiness factor?	Yes **READY**	No (Continue to #2)
2.	Have I researched and identified the education and training requirements for my chosen career field using job postings, official sources, and professionals as resources?	Yes (Continue to #3)	No (Continue to #2a)
	a. I will review several current job postings and identify the typical minimum education and training requirements.	Target Completion Date: Requirements Identified: ☐ Complete; continue to #2b	

Creating Your Individual Development Plan (IDP)

b. If applicable, I will check the following official or regulatory entities and identify the typical minimum education and training requirements:	Target Completion Date: Requirements Identified: ☐ Complete (or N/A); continue to #2c	
c. I will contact the following active professionals for their recommendations regarding education and training requirements:	Target Completion Date: Requirements Identified: ☐ Complete; continue to #3	
3. Have I researched and identified resources that can provide the required education and training?	Yes (Continue to #4)	No (Continue to #3a)
a. I will contact the following educational resources (colleges, organizations, etc.) to determine whether they can provide the required education and training:	Target Completion Date: Education/Training Programs Available: ☐ Complete; continue to #4	
4. Have I made the personal commitment to begin and complete my education and training?	Yes (Continue to #5)	No (See Note A; continue to #5)

95

5.	Do I have the support of my spouse, partner, family, employer, and/or others regarding my decision to complete my education and training?	Yes (Continue to #6)	No (See Note A; continue to #6)
6.	If needed, have I identified and secured any additional resources I may require?	Yes or Not Applicable (Continue to #7)	No (Continue to #6a)
	a. I will identify and secure any additional needed resources. The resources identified include:	Target Completion Date: Additional Resources Secured: ☐ Complete; continue to #7	
7.	Have I successfully applied for and enrolled to begin my education and training?	Yes (Continue to #8)	No (Continue to #7a)
	a. By the date indicated, I will prepare and submit an application for admission to the selected educational or training resource or facility.	Target Completion Date for Submission of Application: ☐ Complete; continue to #7b	
	b. I will begin classes or training by the date indicated.	Target Date to Begin: ☐ Classes/Training Started (Continue to #8)	
8.	I will complete the required education or training by the target date indicated.	Target Date for Completion: ☐ Education and Training Completed *Ready*	
Note A: Without a strong personal commitment on your part and support from others who will be critical to your success, completing your required education and training will be more difficult.			

Creating Your Individual Development Plan (IDP)

INDIVIDUAL DEVELOPMENT PLAN FOR EXPERIENCE

Individual Development Plan for Experience		
1. Does the self-assessment indicate I am ready regarding experience?	Yes **READY**	No (Continue to #2)
2. Have I researched the experience requirements for my chosen career field?	Yes (Continue to #3)	No (Continue to #2a)
a. I will review several current job postings and identify the typically expected experience.	Target Completion Date: Experience Identified: ☐ Complete; continue to #2b	
b. If applicable, I will check the following official or regulatory entities regarding experience requirements:	Target Completion Date: Experience Identified: ☐ Complete; continue to #2c	
c. I will contact the following active professionals for their recommendations regarding experience:	Target Completion Date: Experience Identified: ☐ Complete; continue to #3	
3. Is it possible to obtain the required type and amount of experience in my present position?	Yes (Continue to #3a)	No (Continue to #4)

The Six Readiness Factors for Planning, Changing, or Advancing Your Career

a. I will continue to gain the needed experience through my current position by seeking out those tasks which will be most applicable. These tasks include:	Target Completion Date: ☐ Complete **READY**

4. Is it possible to obtain comparable and acceptable experience through other means (e.g., volunteer work, part-time employment, military, etc.)?	Yes (Continue to #4a)	No (See Note A)
a. I will obtain experience through the following means:	Target Completion Date: ☐ Complete **READY**	

Note A: In your current situation, the inability to obtain experience may render the career goal unattainable. If specific experience is <u>mandatory</u> for entry to the career field and you cannot acquire it with your current employer/position or through other means, it may be necessary to explore other employment options. For example, you may need to consider switching to an entry-level or training position in the desired career field to gain the needed experience. Such positions often require less or no prior experience.

Creating Your Individual Development Plan (IDP)

INDIVIDUAL DEVELOPMENT PLAN FOR SKILLS

	Individual Development Plan for Skills		
1.	Did the self-assessment indicate I am ready regarding skills?	Yes **READY**	No (Continue to #2)
2.	Have I researched the skills and/or abilities requirements for my chosen career field?	Yes (Continue to #3)	No (Continue to #2a)
	a. I will review several current job postings and identify the typically expected skills and/or abilities.	Target Completion Date: Skills/Abilities Identified: ☐ Complete; continue to #2b	
	b. I will contact the following active professionals for their recommendations regarding skills and/or abilities:	Target Completion Date: Skills/Abilities Identified: ☐ Complete; continue to #3	
3.	Is it possible to obtain the specifically required skills and/or abilities in my present job?	Yes (Continue to #3a)	No (Continue to #4)
	a. I will find and use opportunities to develop the specific skills and/or abilities identified in 2a and 2b.	Target Completion Date: ☐ Complete **READY**	
4.	Is it possible to obtain acceptable skills and/or abilities through other means (e.g., additional training, a mentor, volunteer work, part-time employment, military, etc.)?	Yes (Continue to #4a)	No (See Note A)

The Six Readiness Factors for Planning, Changing, or Advancing Your Career

a. I will obtain the skills and/or abilities through the following means:	Target Completion Date: ☐ Complete **READY**
Note A: In your current situation, the inability to obtain the necessary skills may render the career goal unattainable. If specific skills are <u>mandatory</u> for entry to the career field and you cannot acquire them with your current employer/position or through other means, exploring other employment options may be necessary. For example, you may need to consider switching to an entry-level or training position in the desired career field to acquire the needed skills. Such positions often have lesser skills requirements.	

Creating Your Individual Development Plan (IDP)

INDIVIDUAL DEVELOPMENT PLAN FOR CREDENTIALS

Individual Development Plan for Credentials			
1.	Did the self-assessment indicate I am ready regarding credentials?	Yes **READY**	No (Continue to #2)
2.	Have I researched and identified the required credentials for my chosen career field, using job postings, official sources, and professionals as resources?	Yes (Continue to #3)	No (Continue to #2a)
	a. I will review several current job postings and identify the typically expected credentials.	Target Completion Date: Credentials Identified: ☐ Complete; continue to #2b	
	b. If applicable, I will check the following official or regulatory entities regarding required credentials:	Target Completion Date: Credentials Identified: ☐ Complete; continue to #2c	
	c. I will contact the following active professionals for their recommendations regarding credentials:	Target Completion Date: Credentials Identified: ☐ Complete; continue to #3	
3.	Have I researched the requirements and process necessary to obtain the needed credentials and identified any available preparatory resources?	Yes (Continue to #4)	No (Continue to #3a)

	a. I will research the process and requirements necessary to receive the needed credentials.	Target Completion Date: Process and Requirements Identified: ☐ Complete; continue to #3b
	b. I will research the need and availability of resources (e.g., study guides, courses, etc.) that may be helpful.	Target Completion Date: Resources Identified: ☐ Complete; continue to #4
4.	Do I meet the minimum qualifications required to formally apply for the identified credentials?	Yes (Continue to #4b) / No (Continue to #4a)
	a. I will pursue the actions necessary to meet the minimum qualifications required to apply.	Target Completion Date: Actions Identified: ☐ Complete; continue to #4b
	b. I will begin the formal application process for the credentials.	Target Completion Date: ☐ Complete; continue to #5
5.	Have I adequately studied and prepared for any test, exam, or other requirements necessary to obtain the credentials?	Yes (Continue to #6) / No (Continue to #5a)

a. If needed, appropriate, and available, I will obtain and use the resources identified in 3b to aid in preparation.	Target Completion Date: ☐ If complete or not needed, continue to #5b
b. I will schedule time for preparation activities.	Target Completion Date: ☐ Complete; continue to #6
6. I will complete any final requirements and obtain the credentials.	Target Completion Date: ☐ Complete **READY**

INDIVIDUAL DEVELOPMENT PLAN FOR DIFFERENTIATION

Individual Development Plan for Differentiation		
1. Am I satisfied with the Differentiation Readiness Score indicated by the self-assessment?	Yes **READY**	No (Continue to #2)
2. Listed below are the actions relevant to my career field that I will complete to help favorably differentiate myself, including deadlines for completion.		
Action to Be Taken:		Target Completion Date: ☐ Complete
Action to Be Taken:		Target Completion Date: ☐ Complete
Action to Be Taken:		Target Completion Date: ☐ Complete
Action to Be Taken:		Target Completion Date: ☐ Complete
Action to Be Taken:		Target Completion Date: ☐ Complete
Differentiation readiness is a matter of degree. The more ways you can favorably differentiate yourself from the other applicants, the more likely you are to be viewed as a preferred candidate. You are **READY** when you feel you have taken reasonable measures to sufficiently differentiate yourself.		

INDIVIDUAL DEVELOPMENT PLAN FOR INTERVIEWING

	Individual Development Plan for Interviewing		
1.	Did the self-assessment indicate I am ready regarding interviewing?	Yes **READY**	No (Continue)
	Perform any of the following for which the self-assessment indicated improvement was needed.		
2.	I will practice describing aloud my education and training clearly and concisely, without having to continually refer to my resume or other materials. Target Completion Date:		☐ Complete
3.	I will practice describing aloud my applicable work experience and skills clearly and concisely, as they specifically relate to the desired position, without having to continually refer to my resume or other materials. Target Completion Date:		☐ Complete
4.	I will attempt to anticipate work-related questions specific to my field that I am likely to be asked during an interview and practice my responses aloud. Topic areas may include: • Technical • Procedures • Processes • Laws • Regulations • Standards • Equipment • IT • Software • Safety • Clinical • Social Media • Design • Other: Target Completion Date:		☐ Complete
5.	I will research and review generic interview questions, develop answers, and practice my responses aloud. Target Completion Date:		☐ Complete
6.	I will research and review behavioral format interview questions, develop answers, and practice my responses aloud. Target Completion Date:		☐ Complete
7.	If my interview may include a skills test or other demonstration of proficiency, I will prepare as needed. Target Completion Date:		☐ Complete
8.	I will develop, prepare, or update my resume (or CV) and other related materials. Target Completion Date:		☐ Complete
9.	I will obtain unofficial copies of my college (or high school) transcripts and learn the procedure to provide official versions to an employer. Target Completion Date:		☐ Complete
10.	I will review my online presence and social media posts, revising as necessary to help ensure they convey a favorable image. Target Completion Date:		☐ Complete
	Interviewing readiness is a matter of degree. Preparation and practice will result in a less stressful interview and increased chances for success. You are **READY** when you feel you have adequately addressed each of the above.		

Go for It!

Congratulations! It took time and effort, but you have developed your career plan! Now comes the critical part: to execute the plan elements within the deadlines you established. Be careful, however, to avoid a common failure that plagues many strategic plans, whether personal or in the corporate world. That failure is that, although significant time may have been spent creating the plan, it is frequently then "put on the shelf" because other pressing matters arise that always seem to take priority. When this happens, the initial excitement and momentum surrounding the plan fade away. Ultimately, the plan is never carried out. The end result? Nothing changes. Nothing improves.

The fact is, life happens. Something is *always* going to come up, and you have to adjust accordingly, making sure to not lose sight of the end goal or let it overwhelm you. How can you do this?

Do you have a goal of regularly exercising or working out at the gym? If so, how do you accomplish it? Simple; you do it consistently at regular intervals. At first, it might have been challenging and inconvenient. But after a while, it became a habit and a regular part of your daily routine. Your IDP and career goals may not always require daily attention; however, their progress must be periodically reviewed, perhaps monthly or even weekly, especially if you have goals with short time frames.

Carve out a small amount of time, say fifteen or thirty minutes, every month or week at the same time, and review your progress. After a while, like exercising, the periodic review will become a habit and part of your regular routine. Hopefully, most reviews will be simple, short, and conclude with, "Yup, right on target." However, if a review finds you are a bit behind schedule, or have encountered an unexpected roadblock, you can catch it early and resolve the problem before it seriously impacts the plan. The review also provides an opportunity to ensure any upcoming tasks related to a goal are not forgotten and are therefore carried out as planned.

Perhaps one of the best reasons to perform a periodic review is that it can provide an encouraging boost to your morale. As you slowly but surely complete each goal, you will see progress being made. Achievement of your overall career plan will not just be a dream for someday, but reality coming ever closer and within reach!

I once spoke with a highly successful physician about career goals, and he shared his perspective and experiences relating to his many years of college and medical school. Yes, he had an overall plan. However, his short-term goal was always to simply complete the next upcoming class. He avoided being crushed by the enormity of the challenge by focusing only on the next step ahead. He said that had he had stopped to dwell on the work which lay ahead, he could have easily become overwhelmed and dropped out. Instead, he concentrated all his energy on just making it through the next upcoming class. Remember, one bite at a time.

When following through on your own plan, keep your focus on the next item ahead. Don't get overwhelmed. You have already mapped out all the required actions to ensure the plan is complete and nothing will be missed. Now, just take things one step at a time.

At the beginning of this book, I asked if you were ready to make a significant change in your career and life. If you have read this far, performed your self-assessment, and carefully developed your individual development plan, I will take that as a definite "Yes!"

The only thing left to do now is to *go for it!* Best wishes and good luck in achieving your career goals!

Appendix A: Telephone and Online Video Interviews

While telephone and online video interviews do not have the logistical issues involved with physical travel, they do have their own, unique considerations. First, the location of the interview is reversed. The interviewer is, in essence, invited to your turf, either audibly, visually, or both. Second, the technology involved with each of these remote interview types requires special attention.

TELEPHONE INTERVIEWS

Just as with a regular, in-person interview, be on time. If the interviewer is calling you, be ready and waiting at the designated time. If you are placing the call, do not call too early and certainly not late. Phoning a few minutes before the start time should be acceptable; however, use a known, accurate time source, such as your cell phone (if it is correct).

Like they say in the real estate business, location, location, location. Make sure the room you use is quiet and private. No noisy kids, pets, or other people. No music or TV in the background. Does your location regularly have planes or trains passing nearby, or traffic noise and sirens? If so, find somewhere else to make the call. Repeatedly apologizing for distracting noises only tells the interviewer you are a person who fails to plan or pay attention to details.

Regarding the phone itself, make sure the battery is fully charged and the location has reliable reception and signal strength. Do you receive lots of incoming calls or messages? If so, perhaps you can temporarily silence such notifications. Do you have access to a wired landline? You may think it is old school, but using a landline eliminates potential reception and battery problems. Does your phone have a mute button? Know where it is and how to use it in case you unexpectedly need to sneeze or cough. Whatever phone you use, be sure you know how to operate it like an expert. The last thing you want to do is accidentally disconnect the interviewer!

Have a pen and paper handy to take notes. Also, have your resume and other reference materials right in front of you, and be completely familiar with them. You do not want the interviewers to hear you shuffling papers, saying "um," and "er," while trying to look up details.

Since they cannot see you, have some talking points or questions prepared and written for easy reference. However, do not read aloud word-for-word from your notes, as your answers should sound spontaneous.

The beginning of the interview is an excellent time to ask if the interviewers received your application, resume, and other materials. In the event something did not download properly or a file went missing, you could offer to resend it. Usually, they will have everything they need, but this step shows you are courteous and pay attention to detail.

As with any interview, you want to prepare for questions you suspect will be asked, but here, there is a twist. If this is a preliminary phone interview or screening, they are typically not expected to be lengthy, so have the short version of your answers practiced and ready to go. Unless the interviewer wants more detail, keep your answers brief and to the point.

Again, just as you would prepare for an in-person interview, be sure to research the company in advance. They may ask how you learned about the position or whether you are familiar with their organization, so have some brief, positive things to say. If you know little or nothing about them, they might wonder why you even bothered to apply.

In today's text message world, many people are not very good telephone communicators. They just are not comfortable or particularly adept at speaking on the phone. Does that include you? If so, you may come across as timid, shy, bumbling, or ineffective, an impression you certainly do not want to give. If your phone skills could use some improvement, set up some practice interview phone calls with a friend or mentor. The more you practice, the more comfortable and confident you will be, and the words will come more easily and naturally.

Do not eat or have anything in your mouth while on the interview. Chewing or swallowing noises are annoying, plus you would hate to start coughing. Keep some water handy, but only use it if needed. Remember the mute button mentioned earlier? It may come in handy here.

A critical aspect of a telephone interview is that, out of the five senses, only one—hearing—is at play here for both you and the interviewer. Therefore, you will need to listen very carefully. Since you cannot see the interviewer, you will have no visual clues as to whether your answers are well-received. Also, since the interviewer cannot see you, your voice has to do all the work. It must sound pleasant and convey professionalism, confidence, and friendliness.

ONLINE VIDEO INTERVIEWS

Communicating with friends and family via apps such as FaceTime or Zoom is usually an enjoyable experience; however, the thought of an online job interview may be a bit intimidating. After all, your potential career and big dollars are on the line!

Online interviews should be easy, right? You don't have to deal with the hassles typically associated with physical interviews, such as traffic, parking, finding the right office, or maybe even flight schedules and hotels. In reality, those problems may have been exchanged for potential new ones, some of which you may not have even considered yet.

However, before discussing issues specifically related to online interviews, note that everything necessary to prepare for a traditional face-to-face interview also applies. As an applicant, you still need to:

- Dress professionally and appropriately, just as if you were interviewing in person. However, a caveat regarding clothing will be discussed later.
- Do your research so you are knowledgeable about the company. This will help you develop intelligent questions.
- Review the position description or posting again to better understand the job and its duties. This may also lead to questions you will want to ask.
- Try to anticipate some of the questions you may be asked and develop responses.
- Repeatedly practice your responses to expected questions or topics so the words will come more easily. However, try to sound natural and not overly rehearsed.
- Have your resume, cover letter, references, etc. handy in case you need them.
- Be prepared for a skills test either before, during, or after the interview.

Next, some of the challenges specific to online job interviews will be addressed. These will be broken down into four broad categories:

- Location
- Technology
- Photographic Considerations
- On-Camera Conduct

Location

This refers to *your* location; specifically, the physical space in which you will have the interview. Why is location important? Consider this: When you go to a physical interview, where is it usually held? Typically, the employer conducts the interview in a quiet, private conference room or office, free from noise, interruptions, and other distractions. Now, honestly, does your planned interview location (usually your home or apartment) meet those same criteria most of the time? If not, you will need to make some changes to ensure it does, or else change location.

A few years ago, a college professor was giving a live interview on CNN, speaking about the serious topic of North Korea[7]. Suddenly, during the broadcast, two of his very young children burst into the room. Next, his wife entered as well, attempting to round up and remove the toddlers. Again, this all took place on live international television! The clip went viral. This may be funny for us to watch, but not so much for the professor. Imagine your embarrassment if something like that happened during your online job interview! Sure, the prospective employer may be polite and chuckle. However, this situation might be taken as a sign you failed to properly plan for the interview and pay attention to detail.

When deciding on an online interview location, many of the same considerations discussed earlier for telephone interviews are also applicable here. These include:

- Kids and pets must be supervised or removed so they will not unexpectedly join the interview. Barking dogs, loud, chirping birds, or cats that suddenly jump on you may not necessarily be considered cute.
- Make sure anyone else in the home or apartment knows about the interview and will not disturb you. In fact, they can help by watching the kids, pets, or answering the doorbell, etc.
- No music or TV should be playing in the background.
- Does your location regularly have audible traffic noises, passing planes or trains, sirens, etc.? If so, find somewhere else to do the interview.
- Watch for other room noises you may have come to ignore, such as a squeaky ceiling fan or a loud appliance.
- Silence any other phones or devices in the room which may ring or alarm.

Taking these steps avoids trouble and demonstrates that you plan and pay attention to detail. Above all, if something unexpected does happen—as it did to the guy on CNN—keep your cool, go with the flow, and make a good recovery. Show the interviewers you can handle stressful situations with composure!

Technology

Online interviews obviously require technology, both hardware and software. The hardware includes not just your device (laptop, tablet, phone, desktop) but possibly also other equipment, such as a separate webcam, monitor screen, microphone, modem, hotspot device, etc. Software refers to the specific application which will be used to conduct the online interview.

What type of device will you be using—a smartphone, tablet, laptop, or desktop computer? If possible, avoid using your phone for a video interview. Instead, use a device with a larger screen to better see the interviewers. This is particularly helpful when multiple interviewers will be participating. You do not want to be unconsciously squinting or putting your face right up to the screen, trying to see their tiny faces. A larger screen will help you read the interviewers' reactions while answering questions, which may not be possible on a small device.

Consider going into the device settings in advance and, if possible, temporarily disable notifications for texts, emails, applications, etc. It will be hard to focus during an interview if your screen is continuously being flooded with text notifications. Plus, if that occurs, the interviewers will see you are obviously distracted. Worse yet, they may assume you are rudely reading text messages during the interview!

Make sure you know how to expertly operate whatever device is being used. You certainly do not want to accidentally cut off the interviewers while attempting to adjust the volume or make some similar adjustment. Also, test and ensure your camera and microphone are working in advance. If your Wi-Fi connection is sometimes sketchy, consider going to a different location or even using a desktop computer with an Ethernet connection wired to your modem. Not only is a wired setup more stable, but it also offers better security protection from those who may try to hack in on your wireless connection.

The email invitation you received should provide clear instructions on connecting to the interview and the software used. This may be something as simple as FaceTime, Zoom, or Skype, familiar apps you may have used many times. On the other hand, employers may also use commercial software with which you are totally unfamiliar. Again, the email invitation should include specific instructions and a link. Clicking the link will either grant you direct access to the interview site or, in some cases, prompt you to first download a small piece of required software.

Applications used for online interviews typically come in two flavors: generic business meeting software and products designed specifically for job interviews. Generic business meeting software may include commercial products such as Cisco Webex, Microsoft Teams, Adobe Connect, GoToMeeting, or other such applications. Although primarily intended for business meetings and conferences, these packages are also frequently used for interviews because companies already have them and are familiar with their use.

Alternatively, some companies may use software designed specifically for online job interviews. These may include applications such as Spark Hire, VidCruiter, or HireVue, among many others. Often, packages like these may interface directly with human resources software, such as an applicant tracking system (ATS). Interview-specific software may also include features such as skills testing. Some are even designed to conduct a semi-automated "digital interview" in which candidates record video responses to a set of questions. The interviewers then view the recordings later, at their convenience.

Photographic Considerations

Since you are on camera, you want to look your best and make a great visual first impression! To help ensure this happens, consider a few fundamentals professional photographers routinely take into consideration. These include:

- Background
- Lighting
- Camera angle
- Camera-to-subject distance
- Glare
- Clothing

Background

Other than yourself, what else in the room is visible to the camera? Some video podcasters have been known to have piles of dirty laundry clearly stacked on the washing machine behind them. Can any clutter be seen? Do you have posters or pictures in the field of view that may be controversial or considered inappropriate for a job interview?

Also, with apps such as Zoom, forget using those cheesy digital backgrounds. No one will be impressed if you have the Eiffel Tower in your background when they know you live in Kansas. Aside from possibly goofy content, digital backgrounds added by free or low-cost applications often place an unnatural outline or glow around your body, which can look silly and be distracting.

Make sure there are no bright lights visible in the background, particularly windows or lamps. Photographers know that a strong "backlight" causes automatic cameras to underexpose the subject in an attempt to compensate for the overall brightness of the picture (see next page). When this occurs, your face will appear too dark to be seen clearly, and the window or lamp will be overly bright and distracting. Due to automatic adjustment by the camera, whatever is outside the window is often properly exposed and clearly visible, but you are too dark, perhaps even completely silhouetted. The interviewer wants to see you, not your backyard.

Lighting

To look your best, you need to be adequately and nicely lit. The illumination must be soft and even, producing no harsh shadows either on your face or in the background. Avoid bland, straight-on lighting. The light source should be in front and slightly off to the side, but not positioned too high or too low relative to your head. Otherwise, harsh shadows will appear on your face, making you look like an escapee from a horror movie! Also, if the light is too bright, the result will not be flattering. Depending on your complexion or makeup, you may appear shiny or pasty-faced.

What about outdoor lighting? Generally, outside is not the best place for an interview due to numerous uncontrollable factors that could cause havoc. In addition to noise, the weather could create problems (wind, unexpected rain, etc.), bees and other insects or pests could interfere, Wi-Fi reception may be spotty, etc. However, if your patio, porch, or similar location is the only suitable spot, watch the lighting to make sure it is soft and indirect. Avoid harsh, direct sunlight (see below).

Soft and indirect outdoor lighting

Avoid direct and harsh outdoor lighting

Camera Angle

The angle at which the camera is placed can have a profound effect on your appearance. Many people make the mistake of positioning the camera too low relative to their face, causing it to look up at them. The result? Since your chin and neck are then closest to the camera, they may look unnaturally large. Even worse, the interviewer is looking right up your nostrils! Placing the camera slightly above or more even with your face presents a more natural and flattering image (see below).

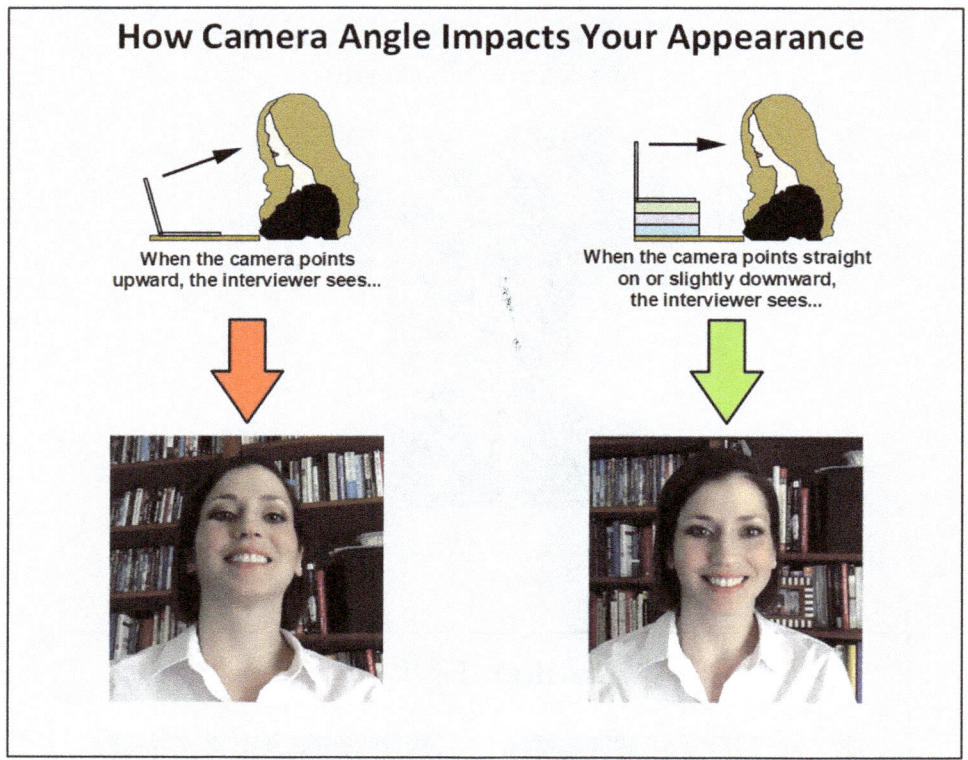

Earlier, we discussed backgrounds. Having the camera pointing upward also opens the door for still more background problems. Got a ceiling fan? If you're not careful, you could end up looking like Inspector Gadget with his helicopter hat! Or, the ceiling light could now be the source of a strong, unwanted backlight.

Camera-to-Subject Distance

When you are too far away from the camera, you will appear tiny to the interviewers on their end. They will be unable to see your face adequately, detracting from the interview. On the other hand, if you are too close, the camera lens may cause a "fish-eye" effect, significantly distorting and enlarging your face, especially your nose. The degree to which this occurs depends on the particular lens in the camera. What to do? Experiment with your device ahead of time and find a distance that provides the best compromise of image size (of you) while maintaining a flattering appearance.

Glare

If you wear glasses, watch for reflections and glare from the device screen or windows. Do you wear glasses with photochromic lenses that darken automatically? Watch they do not darken so much that they conceal your eyes, making it look like you wore sunglasses to the interview. Using FaceTime, Zoom, or some other familiar app, experiment ahead of time to determine if any glare or unwanted reflections are present. While you may not be able to eliminate glare completely, try moving yourself or the camera around to minimize it as much as possible.

Clothing

Of course, you need to dress professionally, just as if you were going to an in-person interview. However, there is something to watch for when it comes to the use of video. Have you ever seen a news anchor or person being interviewed on TV with clothing or a necktie that produced a bizarre, moving, almost psychedelic image? This technically-induced problem is known as a "moiré effect." It is sometimes created when clothing with a fine pattern (such as herringbone) or a certain weave is viewed by a video camera.

To avoid this, wear solid clothing or something with a solid background and avoid checkered or patterned garments. Look at yourself on camera. Does your clothing choice produce this very annoying and distracting effect?

On-Camera Conduct

A few additional details must be considered with online interviews, especially related to your conduct while on camera.

Remember at all times that you are on camera and visible to the interviewers. When in the comfort of your own space, it may be easy to forget and do things you would likely never do during an in-person interview. These might include unconscious habits, such as biting your nails, rolling your eyes at interviewer comments, repeatedly touching your nose or mouth, licking your lips, fidgeting with a pen or other item, and so forth.

Applicants are always encouraged to maintain good eye contact with the interviewers. How do you do that online? To appear as if you are looking at the interviewers, you must look directly into the camera lens. However, when you do that, you probably will be unable to see the screen and therefore unable to judge the reactions of the interviewers. The best solution is to maintain a balance. For example, when beginning your response to a question, look directly into the camera. Doing this gives the appearance on their end that you are looking at the interviewers. But since you want to read their reactions, glance away from the camera occasionally and look at the screen. To make this easier and seem more natural, practice this technique with a friend in advance.

One advantage of an online interview is you can have notes or other materials handy, so long as you keep them out of view of the camera. For example, quickly write down the interviewers' names on a card or sheet of paper and place it where only you can see it. This way, you can refer to it as needed without having to rely solely on your memory. With a little practice, you can make this look natural. While it is fine to have a few notes handy, avoid overdoing it. Continually looking down at such materials will make it appear as if you are unfamiliar with your material. After all, you should already know the content of your resume from memory, and anything entered on your application. You want to seem quick and sharp, not someone who has to refer to their notes for every little thing.

Just as arriving on time for an in-person interview is a given, the same is true for an online interview. In fact, check into the link a few minutes early. First, this demonstrates you are punctual. Second, if you need to address any unexpected or last-minute technology glitches, you can hopefully resolve them before the interview start time.

PRACTICE

Finally, one of the biggest takeaways regarding online interviews is that the best way to prepare is to practice. Use your favorite video app and conduct a mock interview with a friend or mentor. Provide them with questions to ask and practice responding on camera. They can also offer useful feedback regarding room appearance, audible noises, your on-camera habits, eye contact, camera angle, etc.

Appendix B: Sample Behavioral Questions

Candidates frequently struggle to answer behavioral interview questions. This may be due to unfamiliarity with the question format, lack of preparation, or both. If one is unaccustomed to such questions and has not considered answers in advance, the interview stress can make it difficult to quickly recall relevant experiences. Consequently, rather than describing a specific situation in detail, as the interviewer was seeking, candidates tend to provide vague responses. Of course, this means they failed to answer the question sufficiently and left the interviewer unimpressed.

The number of potential behavioral questions is limitless, so no book, website, or other resources can ever prepare you 100% for what you will be asked. Fortunately, however, behavioral questions typically fall into a limited number of general categories, including but not limited to:

- Teamwork
- Conflict
- Problem Solving
- Customer Service
- Cultural Diversity
- Multitasking/Stress
- Honesty/Integrity
- Judgement/Resourcefulness
- Leadership/Management

Review the sample questions in each of the various categories in advance. By doing so, the situations you recall may be adaptable to any number of behavioral format questions. Formulate your answers using the STAR method presented in an earlier chapter. Again, repeatedly practice your responses aloud to become more comfortable when answering such questions.

TEAMWORK

- Describe a time you were a member of a work team. What was your role? What was the outcome?

- Describe a time you were a member of a work team and one of the members did not cooperate or participate as they should. What did you do and what was the outcome?

- Describe a time you were asked to assemble or lead a work team to accomplish an important task or work on an important project. What did you do and what was the outcome?

CUSTOMER SERVICE

- Describe a time you provided good customer service above and beyond what was normally expected.

- Describe a time you had to interact with an irate or unreasonable customer. What was the situation, what did you do, and what was the outcome?

HONESTY/INTEGRITY

- Describe a time you made a mistake. What happened, what did you do, and what was the outcome?

- Describe a time when a project you undertook failed. What happened, why did it fail, what did you do, and what was the outcome?

- Describe a time when you were called upon to perform a task which, in your opinion, was not in the best interest of the customer or company. What did you do?

CONFLICT

- Describe a time when you had to interact with a coworker who was angry or upset. What did you do and what was the outcome?

- Describe a time when you had to interact with a supervisor or manager who you felt was unreasonable in their directives. What did you do and what was the outcome?

CULTURAL DIVERSITY

- Describe a time you had to work with a person who had a very different cultural background from your own.

- Describe a time when you encountered a language or other communication barrier when working with a customer or coworker. What did you do?

JUDGEMENT/RESOURCEFULNESS/PROBLEM SOLVING

- Describe a time when you needed to make an immediate decision and a supervisor or manager was not available to consult. What did you do and what was the outcome?

- Describe a time when you needed to complete a task but did not have all the necessary resources. What did you do and what was the outcome?

- Describe a time when you, on your own initiative, undertook action to improve something that you knew needed to be improved or corrected. What did you do and what was the outcome?

MULTITASKING/STRESS

- Describe a time when you were given multiple tasks to perform and told they were all a priority. However, you knew not all the tasks could be completed in the requested time frame. What did you do and what was the outcome?

- Describe a time when multiple individuals gave you multiple high-priority tasks to perform in a short amount of time. How did you prioritize them? What was the outcome?

- Describe a time when you became extremely stressed. What did you do and how successful were you at overcoming the stress?

LEADERSHIP/MANAGEMENT

- Describe a time when you had to take charge of a situation or work team which you knew was otherwise not going to be successful. What did you do and what was the outcome?

- Describe a time when you had to fire someone or issue a severe disciplinary action.

- Describe a time when you had to motivate an employee who was not producing at the expected level. What did you do and what was the outcome?

- Describe a time when you had to oversee a situation involving two employees who did not get along but needed to work together to accomplish a specific task or complete a project. How did you handle this situation and what was the outcome?

- Describe a time when you had to announce, support, and enforce a management decision that was not popular with employees and with which you personally may not have agreed.

ATTITUDES ABOUT WORK AND SELF

With these questions, the interviewer is seeking to discover your attitudes and feelings about work or to identify weaknesses or skills needing improvement. The questions may not be situational like the usual behavioral ones, and a STAR answer may not be required. However, when developing your responses, consider how they might be interpreted by someone who does not know you. Examples of such questions include:

- Everyone brings both strengths and weaknesses to a job. What do you believe is your greatest strength as well as your greatest weakness?

- What part of your job do you find the least interesting or satisfying?

- If you could change one aspect of your current job, what would it be?

- What do you feel has been the most significant accomplishment of your professional life?

- If you knew back then what you know now, would you still have chosen to work in this field?

- Everyone needs improvement in some aspect of their skill set or work performance. What specifically do you believe could be improved?

When answering questions of this nature, too much openness or honesty could actually be problematic. It may be best to construct your answer around something fairly benign and choose a so-called weakness that the employer will likely not see as a serious flaw. You might be able to spin your response such that it reinforces how you are always looking to further develop your existing skills. For example:

The interviewer asks: *"Is there any software with which you would like to improve your skill level?"*

A WRONG answer: *"I have real trouble with some advanced financial functions in Excel. I never can seem to get the stupid things to work properly, and I'm never sure how to interpret the results, or if the output is even right. I guess I need improvement in that area."*

A better answer: *"Although I already utilize and am very comfortable with many of Excel's advanced financial functions, I always feel there is room to learn even more. Plus, I enjoy learning new spreadsheet tools."*

The better answer lets you convey that you already know and use several advanced functions. At the same time, it enables you to humbly acknowledge you may not be familiar with them all. You summarize by indicating that you would enjoy learning even more functions, which most people would agree is a positive attribute.

Appendix C: Negotiating a Starting Salary

Success! You applied for a new position, went through an interview (maybe even several), and now have an actual job offer. Like most successful applicants, you are thrilled and excited. However, you might be thinking the starting pay offered should be, well, a bit higher. What do you do now? You may be very skilled in your particular line of work, but negotiating salary might be way outside your comfort zone. Plus, you don't want to appear ungrateful or mess up this opportunity over a few dollars, right?

Relax. Negotiating an acceptable starting salary is usually just a normal part of the overall employment process. Nobody is going to be shocked or appalled if you try to bump up that dollar amount—so long as you do it reasonably and professionally.

The interviewer and Human Resources (HR) department have a duty to find and hire the best possible employees at the lowest reasonable cost. Most employers expect some amount of salary negotiations to take place. Therefore, they might lowball the first salary offer a bit to allow wiggle room to offer more... if you ask. This way, in the end, you feel like you negotiated a great salary deal, and they are happy with what they have to pay. A win-win!

Should you have discussed pay earlier, back during the interview? No, probably not. Unless an interviewer begins actual salary negotiations, it is usually best to wait until a position is offered. Think of it this way: When the employer finally decides they want YOU out of all the other applicants, you gain some negotiating leverage. They have invested time and money to find exactly the person they want to hire. Now, like you, they don't want the deal to fall apart over a few bucks.

During the job interview, be careful to not confuse obligation with negotiation. For various reasons, some organizations require their interviewers to mention the usual starting pay or pay range. They might say something like, "The Analyst II position has a pay level of $28.50 per hour." Such a statement is typically NOT an invitation to begin salary negotiations right then and there. It may just be a requirement the interviewer must follow.

Being successful at negotiating a higher starting salary also depends on what you bring to the table and offer the employer. Consider an entry-level position requiring little or no experience and only modest educational requirements. If you meet only the bare minimum requirements, you really have little negotiating power, as you offer nothing more than any other qualified cookie-cutter applicant. Plus, the other similarly qualified candidates might gladly accept the offered starting pay—and the employer knows it.

On the other hand, when you bring valuable experience, skills, or education beyond the minimum requirements, which other applicants do not likely possess, you become more desirable to the employer. When that is the case, can you justify asking for a higher starting wage? Yes, sometimes you can. If the organization values the extra qualifications you possess and wants those on board, they should be willing to pay more than the minimum—within reason, of course. So, what is reasonable?

It is important to do your homework and carefully research the current job market salary for the position you seek. Without doing so, how will you even know whether the dollar amount being offered is fair and reasonable? Suppose they offer $44,000 per year, and you were thinking $75,000. In this situation, one or perhaps both of the parties obviously have very unrealistic expectations. You may have heard the expression, "knowledge is power." Having a solid knowledge of the going salary rate for similar positions in your industry and in your geographic area provides just that power.

How do you determine a market wage rate for someone in your field? Below are a few resources to aid in your research.

The U.S. Bureau of Labor Statistics (BLS) provides an enormous amount of wage data on over 800 occupations on their website at https://www.bls.gov/oes/current/oes_nat.htm. Find the occupational title that most closely matches the job of interest, click on it, and you will be presented with:

- A profile of which industries hire individuals in that occupation
- Mean hourly and annual wage rates for that occupation
- The number of individuals employed in this occupation, by state
- Annual mean wages for this occupation, by state
- Considerable other statistical data regarding the occupation

While the BLS data can be very helpful and informative, keep the following caveats in mind:

- Wage data are estimates calculated using data collected from employers in the industry sectors
- The information shown may be one or more years old (check the date indicated)
- Wage rates can and do vary significantly by geographic location, including by cities within a state

When searching online for wage information, you may come across the term "prevailing wage." A prevailing wage rate is defined as the average wage paid to similarly employed workers in a specific occupation in the area of intended employment.[8] This term refers specifically to the government-approved wage rates employers must pay when participating in government contracts. The requirement to use a prevailing wage is intended to prevent bid price undercutting through the use of non-union or foreign workers. Important: the typical wages paid to employees engaged in regular employment, i.e., non-government contract work, may or may not be similar to the official prevailing wage rate.

Other resources may provide even more reliable and up-to-date information regarding wage rates, especially for jobs in your immediate vicinity. These include:

- Job postings for positions of interest, some of which may indicate pay ranges
- Individuals already working in the jobs of interest who will often also know the approximate pay ranges offered by employers in the area
- Local bargaining units or union hall (if the job is typically unionized); the representatives may be willing to share their current wage rates
- Various online resources, including job search sites

Once you have this information, but before throwing salary numbers around, make sure you know what you are talking about and have realistically assessed your desirability as a candidate. Then, just as in poker, you must try to read the other party. Can you get a sense of when they have reached their limit? At the same time, you must also know your own limit. At what point are you willing to turn down a job due to a weak salary offer? You will negotiate with more confidence, think more clearly, and experience less stress if you consider such decisions in advance.

Negotiations are all fine and well, but keep in mind most employers have limits and restrictions placed on them. The person you are negotiating with may or may not have the authority to decide the final starting pay level. Almost every position everywhere has an established pay range, low to high. Pay ranges are usually tiered in increments (often called *steps*) based on factors such as years on the job. The starting salary will be somewhere within that range.

The hiring manager may have some wiggle room within the low range of the pay scale, but it is not uncommon for the Human Resources department to have the final say. Not all managers are good negotiators, so HR may require justification before you can be offered a higher starting salary. The hiring manager may even ask you for additional time to discuss the matter with HR; that is normal. HR departments are obligated to ensure salaries are reasonable compared to the job market, are handled equitably throughout the company, and are not in some way discriminatory. Heavily unionized organizations may have bargaining contract restrictions regarding pay that the employer must also observe.

Starting pay flexibility may also be limited when applying for a promotional opportunity with your current employer. HR departments often use a prescribed formula to calculate the new pay level for someone transferring internally to a higher-level position. In this case, there may be less room for negotiation.

Then, there is the matter of the budget. Management at organizations develops and approves an annual salary budget, assigning dollar amounts to every position. Do not be surprised if that budgeted dollar amount is used as a negotiating tactic to avoid initially offering more money. The employer may try the excuse, "Oh, we only budgeted $46,000 for that position, so I don't see how we could possibly offer the $48,000 you are asking." In reality, if an organization has a large number of employees and the overall budget for salaries is sizable, there is almost always some wiggle room. A mutually acceptable compromise should be possible, especially if the pay difference is relatively small.

Do salary negotiations always work? No, of course not. Every situation is different, as are the negotiating skills of each interviewer and candidate. Things can go either way for any number of reasons. One time, I received a job offer for a position I really wanted, but the salary was just too low. Despite my efforts to negotiate, the employer would not budge from the initial offer. Not even a penny. So, I declined the job. What a disappointment! However, turning down that job was the best thing I ever did. I kept searching for a similar position and soon after found one with better pay that also opened the door to many more future opportunities. Another time, I was offered a position and pushed back a little on the initial pay offer, citing my experience and other qualifications as justification. In this case, the employer responded with a new offer considerably higher than I expected. One thing is for sure: if you merely accept the first salary offer, that is all you will get.

Base salary is a prime consideration, but also look at the compensation package as a whole. Do not get too hung up on the per-hour or per-year salary dollars alone. Benefits may play a significant role in the offer. For example, suppose the benefits package with the new employer results in a significantly smaller deduction from your paycheck for healthcare insurance compared to your current coverage. In this case, you could see an increase in take-home pay, just as if you had negotiated a higher wage.

Some companies offer incredibly attractive 401k or similar programs with generous matching funds. Employers often have their available benefits packages already defined; if so, these may not be negotiable. Others may be "cafeteria-style" programs where the employee can pick and choose from a menu of benefit options, so long as the total value selected does not exceed some predefined limit. Regardless of format, a substantial benefits package may be a sound reason to accept a slightly lower per-hour or annual salary amount than you had initially targeted.

Perhaps you really are worth more than the current offer. Plus, although it may be uncomfortable, maybe you are even willing to try negotiating a higher starting salary. But you are likely not a professional negotiator unless your job happens to involve that skill. On the other hand, unlike you, the company representative may be experienced and skilled at negotiating salaries with applicants all the time. How do you pull this off?

First, you must separate yourself from the personal, emotional aspects of the conversation. Doing so is critical! Think of this like any other business discussion, even though it is about you. You must remain objective, polite, and professional. Keep your voice cool and calm, but speak with confidence. Although each of you may push back a little—that is how negotiations work—neither side should try to threaten or bully. If the professionalism breaks down, the negotiations are over and will fail.

Before entering into salary negotiations, give some thought—and practice—as to the actual words you might use. By developing and rehearsing these in advance, they will come easier when you engage in the actual discussions. This will help you remain calm, less stressed and nervous, and better able to focus.

For example, suppose the negotiator offers nothing more than the usual, entry-level starting wage. However, you know for a fact that given your qualifications, the offer is way too low. Before speaking, choose your words carefully and keep your tone neutral. You do not want to sound unappreciative, offended, angry, or pushy. Also, do not phrase your statement in a yes/no question format to which the negotiator might simply say "No," or "We couldn't do that." Instead, express your salary concern in an open-ended manner so as to open the door for more discussion. In this situation, you might politely but firmly say something (using your own words) to the effect of:

> *"I understand your salary offer is consistent with your company's usual starting wage. However, as my education and work experience exceed the minimum requirements for this position, I believe a higher starting wage would be appropriate."*

Then be quiet. The negotiator heard your polite dissatisfaction with the initial offer, and now the ball is back in their court. They need to make the next move and sweeten the deal.

The negotiator may respond with, "Well, what salary did you have in mind?" I suggest not answering with an exact number right away, as whatever you indicate may be too high or even lower than what they may be willing to offer. For your first counteroffer, perhaps propose a range, such as, "I was thinking something in the mid-40s would be reasonable." This response provides a solid idea of your target amount and still offers wiggle room the negotiator may legitimately need.

The negotiator may then counter with a specific amount, such as, "We could offer the third-year rate of $43,500, and you would be eligible for another raise after one year. Would that work for you?" The ball is back in your court. What do you do? Accept the offer, attempt to negotiate further, or politely walk away from the job offer altogether? This where knowing your salary boundaries in advance is vital.

Important points to remember regarding salary negotiations:

- Recognize that starting pay negotiation is a normal part of the hiring process.
- Accept that you will likely need to engage in such negotiations.
- Wait to discuss salary until you have bargaining power, such as when an actual job offer is on the table.
- Know your actual desirability as a candidate.
- Do your homework and know the market pay rates in your field and geographic area.
- Receiving a job offer is exciting, but do not let it cloud your judgment. Know your bottom dollar limit and at what point you are willing to walk away from an unacceptable salary offer.
- Recognize that, while hiring managers and employers have budget limits and authority levels, they also usually have some flexibility. They may need time to get approval to offer higher pay.
- Keep the negotiations polite, professional, and objective at all times.
- When deciding whether a starting salary is acceptable, look at the compensation package as a whole.
- Think about and practice what you will say in advance so you are less nervous and the words come easier.
- Consider that salary negotiation may not always be successful strictly in terms of dollars, but if you are happy with the final offer, you still win.

To be ready before going into an interview or discussing salary when offered a position, make sure you have:

- ➢ Researched market wages for the position and determined what would constitute a competitive salary offer.
- ➢ Taken into account the geographic area for the actual job location. Wages can and do vary greatly by region, state, or even city.
- ➢ Developed and practiced talking points to use if you need to engage in salary negotiations.
- ➢ Considered your boundaries for salary and benefits.
- ➢ Decided on the dollar amount below which you will politely decline an offer.

REFERENCES

1. Hipple, Steven F., Hammond, Laurel A., "Self-employment in the United States," U.S. Bureau of Labor Statistics, March 2016. https://www.bls.gov/spotlight/2016/self-employment-in-the-united-states/home.htm

2. "Number of Employers Using Social Media to Screen Candidates at All-Time High, Finds Latest CareerBuilder Study," http://press.careerbuilder.com/2017-06-15-Number-of-Employers-Using-Social-Media-to-Screen-Candidates-at-All-Time-High-Finds-Latest-CareerBuilder-Study

3. Newport, Frank, "The New Era of Communication Among Americans," Gallop, (2014), https://news.gallup.com/poll/179288/new-era-communication-americans.aspx.

4. Grossbard, Jason, "SMS Marketing Statistics 2021 For USA Businesses," SMS Comparison, (2021), https://www.smscomparison.com/mass-text-messaging/2021-statistics/.

5. Rick, Scott I., Maurice E. Schweitzer, "The imbibing idiot bias: Consuming alcohol can be hazardous to your (perceived) intelligence," Science Direct, Journal of Consumer Psychology, Volume 23, Issue 2 (2013): 212-219, https://www.sciencedirect.com/science/article/abs/pii/S1057740812000927.

6. Lipnic, Victoria A., "The State of Age Discrimination and Older Workers in the U.S. 50 Years After the Age Discrimination in Employment Act (ADEA)," U.S. Equal Employment Opportunity Commission, June 2018, https://www.eeoc.gov/reports/state-age-discrimination-and-older-workers-us-50-years-after-age-discrimination-employment.

7. "Kids Interrupt Dad's Live TV Interview," CNN, March 2017, https://www.cnn.com/videos/world/2017/03/10/interview-interrupted-children-newday.cnn.

8. "Prevailing Wages," U.S. Department of Labor, accessed May 10, 2021, https://www.dol.gov/agencies/eta/foreign-labor/wages/prevailing-wage.

ABOUT THE AUTHOR

Donald Whiteside has thirty years of professional management experience in a broad range of areas, including Biomedical Engineering, State Government, Facilities Management, Radiology, Nuclear Medicine, Radiologic Technology Education, as well as other fields. He has an MBA degree from the University of Michigan-Flint, holds various certifications and licenses, and is a Fellow of the American College of Healthcare Executives (ACHE). Whiteside has presented at national conferences and received awards for his work in technology management. Additionally, he has managed employee development programs, taught courses in business management and biomedical technology at three different colleges, and authored various articles for small publications. In 2017, Whiteside founded CareerLantern.com, a website providing discussion and insight into various career-related topics. In 2019, he launched, produced, and began hosting the popular Career Lantern podcast series. Don is an avid musician, amateur radio operator, and photographer, and resides with his wife in Michigan.